Formerly
New Directions for
Mental Health Services

S0-BFC-742

Gil G. Noam
Editor-in-Chief

NEW DIRECTIONS FOR YOUTH DEVELOPMENT

Theory
Practice
Research

summer | 2002

Youth Development and After-School Time

A Tale of Many Cities

Gil G. Noam
Beth M. Miller | *editors*

JOSSEY-BASS
A Wiley Company
www.josseybass.com

Youth Development and After-School Time
Gil G. Noam, Beth M. Miller (eds.)
New Directions for Youth Development, No. 94, Summer 2002
Gil G. Noam, Editor-in-Chief

Microfilm copies of issues and articles are available in 16mm and 35mm, as well as microfiche in 105mm, through University Microfilms Inc., 300 North Zeeb Road, Ann Arbor, Michigan 48106-1346.

ISSN 1533-8916 (print)   ISSN 1537-5781 (online)   ISBN 0-7879-6337-2 (print)

New Directions for Youth Development is part of The Jossey-Bass Psychology Series and is published quarterly by Wiley Subscription Services, Inc., a Wiley company, at Jossey-Bass, 989 Market Street, San Francisco, California 94103-1741. Periodicals postage paid at San Francisco, California, and at additional mailing offices. Postmaster: Send address changes to New Directions for Youth Development, Jossey-Bass, 989 Market Street, San Francisco, California 94103-1741.

Subscriptions cost $70.00 for individuals and $135.00 for institutions, agencies, and libraries. Prices subject to change. Refer to the order form at the back of this issue.

Editorial correspondence should be sent to the Editor-in-Chief, Dr. Gil G. Noam, Harvard Graduate School of Education, Larsen Hall 601, Appian Way, Cambridge, MA 02138 or McLean Hospital, 115 Mill Street, Belmont, MA 02478.

Cover photograph by Getty Images.

Jossey-Bass Web address: www.josseybass.com

Manufactured in the United States of America on acid-free recycled paper containing at least 20 percent postconsumer waste.

Contents

Editor's Notes

Youth development and after-school time

FEW OTHER ISSUES in youth development receive as much attention and funding today as organized out-of-school time. The new federal education bill has made $1 billion in provisions for after-school programming to be administered throughout the fifty states. Many creative programs have sprung up, large-scale evaluations of program efficacy are under way, and training opportunities are increasing. It is indeed a creative and productive time, as many institutions, collaboratives, and individuals are coming together to shape the risky hours when school is out and parents are still at work. There is public resolve to make the latchkey phenomenon a thing of the past and to give children and youth a rich, fun, and educational experience in after-school settings.

This issue of *New Directions for Youth Development* looks at exciting citywide and cross-city initiatives in after-school time. Not surprisingly, the most interesting efforts occur at the local level, where community-based organizations, museums, universities, schools, and clinics are joining forces, sharing funding and other resources, and jointly creating a system of after-school care and education. Cities have the capacity to create broad collaborations and share intellectual and financial resources. Cities also have the responsibility to provide tens of thousands of children, adolescents, and families with organized after-school activities. In addition, it is at the local level that after-school time has become synonymous with youth development, a way of understanding young people and their needs and a way of interacting with tens of thousands of

NEW DIRECTIONS FOR YOUTH DEVELOPMENT, NO. 94, SUMMER 2002 © WILEY PERIODICALS, INC.

children and adolescents. Good urban after-school education could represent youth development at its best, breeding a city environment that is safe and open, full of exploratory learning and other positive possibilities.

It is with this potential in mind that I invited my colleague Beth Miller, a leader in the field of after-school, to edit an early issue of New Directions in Youth Development on this topic. I have worked over the years with two creative citywide after-school initiatives—one in Boston and one in New York—and have been fortunate to observe firsthand the amazing progress made in both of these urban worlds and to contribute to their efforts.

Outside the circle of policymakers and providers, few people know the depth and breadth of this work or have a finger on the pulse of the exciting initiatives throughout the country. Clearly, a report is needed—one that captures the progress of a few exemplary cities and some cross-city initiatives. The case studies assembled here represent youth development work that combines large-scale policymaking, developmental thinking, and innovative programming, as well as research and evaluation. We could not include every innovation, such as foundation-based initiatives from DeWitt Wallace and the Robert Wood Johnson Foundation, or every innovative city, such as Seattle, Los Angeles, Denver, Kansas City, and many more, and we will return to the topic of after-school time throughout the life of this journal. This issue represents a starting point, a status report of sorts, illustrating some tangible progress in the field and its vital role in youth development.

Gil G. Noam
Editor-in-Chief

Executive Summary

Chapter One: Youth development and afterschool time: Policy and programming in large cities

Gil G. Noam, Beth M. Miller, Susanna Barry

The expansion of financial and civic support for afterschool programming has created growth in the field and an emphasis on coordination among many agencies and entities. This is particularly true for major cities, where the infrastructure is being built to sustain coordinated citywide networks of afterschool opportunities. These afterschool programs can provide intermediary spaces for young people, that is, nontraditional, noninstitutional environments, where they can participate in decision making and explore new interests. This expansion of afterschool programs and citywide networks raises issues of sustainability and professional development in the afterschool field.

Chapter Two: The long-term sustainability of afterschool programs: The After-School Corporation's strategy

Lucy N. Friedman, Mary S. Bleiberg

Since its inception in 1998, The After-School Corporation (TASC) has worked to create a critical mass of effective after-school programs that generate the public demand and political will needed to transform after-school into a universally available public institution in New York City and State, and eventually across the nation.

NEW DIRECTIONS FOR YOUTH DEVELOPMENT, NO. 94, SUMMER 2002 © WILEY PERIODICALS, INC.

TASC has identified a set of core elements that form a model of a high-quality, affordable, and replicable after-school program. To operate and fund programs, TASC has built an expansive network of public and private partnerships. It manages and blends a diversity of public and private funding streams with the goal of making after-school programs a public responsibility—financially sustainable and universally available to every public school student. As an intermediary between after-school programs and an array of partners, TASC operates as a broker and a buffer to facilitate the operation and funding of programs. In addition, by representing a wide range of constituencies, TASC can advocate effectively on behalf of the after-school movement. TASC also works to broaden the base of information about what works in after-school programs through research and dissemination of promising practices.

As the after-school movement gains momentum, TASC is grappling with several issues that complicate the long-term sustainability of after-school programs. It needs to determine if and how its program model may be modified to reach a greater number of students and communities. In turn, the challenge of preserving quality across more programs raises the question of whether to form a set of standards for after-school programs. TASC also must reflect on how its role must evolve as the after-school initiative matures.

Chapter Three: Positive youth development initiatives in Chicago

Renae Ogletree, Tony Bell, Natasha K. Smith

What is Chicago doing to support young people when they are not in school? What are the gaps? Who are stakeholders involved in out-of-school programming, and what can they do, individually and collectively, to improve that programming? What will it take to build a web of supports for young people throughout their waking hours, throughout the first two decades of their lives, that helps them develop across a range of outcomes?

These are challenging questions for any municipality, especially a city as unique, complex, and large as Chicago. Meeting the needs of the nearly one million children and young people in Chicago who look for services, supports, and opportunities that help them grow and learn is a remarkable challenge. Yet it is clear in this chapter that Chicago is committed to improving out-of-school supports for young people and that the city is positioned to change the odds for its youth.

This chapter explores the growing array of programs, initiatives, organizations, and institutions focused on the out-of-school hours in Chicago.

Chapter Four: Schools alone are not enough: After-school programs and education reform in Boston

Jennifer Davis, David A. Farbman

This chapter reviews the history of the effort in Boston to expand after-school programs and build their capacity to support the standards-based education reforms of the city's public schools. After a brief description of the landscape of the Boston Public Schools and the field of after-school programming in the city, the chapter details the key steps taken toward this goal by the mayor and the office he created to assist the after-school field, the Boston 2:00-to-6:00 After-School Initiative. The chapter also reviews two major initiatives taken by the city's civic and political leadership that sought (and are seeking) to increase the number of children served by and improve the learning that takes place in after-school programs. Finally, the authors describe the challenges and successes of a pilot program created to bridge the gap between the work going on during the school day and that in after-school programs to raise the achievement of academically at-risk students. They conclude that the city's leadership has shown strong commitment to the issue of after-school programming and has expressed a vision that values innovative approaches to enhance learning; nevertheless, much more work remains in order to bring about the full implementation of this vision.

Chapter Five: Building the San Francisco Beacons

Sue Eldredge, Sam Piha, Jodi Levin

In 1994, an influential group of youth advocates brought together public school and city officials, private foundation officers, and directors of neighborhood service organizations to create a new citywide initiative that would foster youth development on a large scale in San Francisco. This chapter describes how the Beacons Initiative's managing intermediary, Community Network for Youth Development, used a theory of change process to forge consensus among a broad range of stakeholders. This process, which drew on information from stakeholders to develop a mission and vision for the initiative, addressed the most immediate challenges and created a road map that would guide this large collaborative toward its long-term goals. The chapter begins with a snapshot of the San Francisco Beacon Centers as they currently exist and then looks back on the collaborative theory of change process that guided their development.

Chapter Six: San Diego's 6 to 6: A community's commitment to out-of-school time

Deborah Ferrin, Steven Amick

San Diego is the first major city in the nation to provide free before- and after-school services to every public elementary and middle school within its borders. This effort went to scale in an extraordinarily short period of time and was supported by the city's history of community collaboration. Evaluations have shown increased test scores, lower crime rates, and high satisfaction among stakeholders.

Chapter Seven: Out-of-school-time programs: At a critical juncture

Joyce Shortt

The growth of interest in out-of-school time has been accompanied by a rise in expectations about what might be accomplished during these hours. Evaluations show positive outcomes for children and youth, and communities are increasingly working together to develop coordinated programming. A significant challenge in the field is the attraction and retention of a committed and competent workforce, which is crucial to building the infrastructure that will sustain large citywide efforts.

Chapter Eight: The various roles of municipal leaders

Mark Ouellette, John E. Kyle

An estimated eight million children between the ages of five and fourteen go home to an empty house on a regular basis. Many of these children are left alone for as many as four hours a day. For cities and towns across America, these unsupervised hours after school ends mean both heightened risk and missed opportunities. Leadership from municipal officials is usually required to forge a communitywide strategy that works for all children. Municipal officials can play an important role in developing a communitywide after-school system and serve as catalysts for far-reaching efforts that address key challenges: promoting partnerships, building public will, assessing local resources and needs, improving quality, broadening access, and developing financing strategies.

Chapter Nine: Ensuring quality and sustainability in after-school programs

An-Me Chung, Adriana A. de Kanter, Robert M. Stonehill

Beginning in 1997, the Charles Stewart Mott Foundation and the U.S. Department of Education began a unique public-private partnership to support the 21st Century Community Learning Centers, a school reform initiative based in schools and designed to provide academic support, learning opportunities, and mentoring to children and youth after school. Federal funds focus on direct service, while foundation funds focus on quality issues. This partnership strives to capitalize on the assets and flexibility of philanthropy and the breadth of a major federal program.

This chapter reviews the issues associated with the growth of after-school programming and the impact on major urban centers.

1

Youth development and afterschool time: Policy and programming in large cities

Gil G. Noam, Beth M. Miller, Susanna Barry

"THE REVOLUTION begins at 3:00 P.M.," Jodi Wilgoren wrote in the *New York Times* in January 2000. "The explosion of after-school programs . . . represents nothing less than the reimagining of the school day for the first time in generations."[1] Indeed, few other current social movements are associated with the same confluence of supporting factors as the organization of afterschool time.[2] One key factor to its significance is its sheer quantity: children spend about 80 percent of their waking hours outside school. While our experience of school typically provides ample memories of long hours spent behind desks, the reality is that school time inhabits only a fraction of children's social, educational, and recreational lives.

In addition, education reform, changes in welfare laws, and the growth of prevention services for youth have played a role in bringing afterschool to the fore. Leaders in education, school-age child care, mental health, juvenile justice, youth development, arts and

Portions of this article were adapted from "The Promise of After-School Programs," by Beth M. Miller, *Educational Leadership*, April 2001, Volume 56, Number 7. Reprinted with permission from ASCD. All rights reserved.

NEW DIRECTIONS FOR YOUTH DEVELOPMENT, NO. 94, SUMMER 2002 © WILEY PERIODICALS, INC.

culture, faith-based organizations, recreation and sports, and other fields have also made concerted efforts to promote the positive potential represented by the afterschool hours. This is especially noticeable in our nation's cities, many of which have embarked on comprehensive afterschool initiatives.

The scope of afterschool care and education

In recent years, civic and financial support for afterschool has snowballed, with a 2001 survey showing that 94 percent of U.S. voters believe that children and teenagers should have organized activities or places to go after school every day that provide opportunities to learn.[3] New funding streams for afterschool programs have been growing at an amazingly fast pace. For example, funding for the federal Department of Education's 21st Century Community Learning Centers program, which provides three-year grants to schools, increased from $1 million in fiscal year 1997 during the Clinton administration to over $800 million less than five years later and to $1 billion under the 2002 reauthorized Elementary and Secondary Education Act. The states will receive much of the 21st Century funds, a welcome development at the time when state budget cuts are beginning to affect the afterschool arena.

Growth of the field

By 1991, there were at least fifty thousand school-age child care programs across the United States serving an estimated 1.7 million children.[4] As the chapters in this volume attest, over the past few years, the support for organizing the unaccounted-for hours after school has accelerated, and as a result thousands of children are being served in major cities. According to a survey released in September 2001 by the National Association of Elementary School Principals, 67 percent of principals saw their schools offer optional afterschool programs. Programs like these are often sponsored by a heterogeneous assembly of providers, including Y's, Boys and Girls Clubs, proprietary child care chains, community education departments, grassroots organizations, parent-run nonprofits, and faith organizations.

As the number of programs has grown, so must the field evolve in legitimacy and quality. Many organizations, from the National Academy of Sciences to small youth development and family support groups, have become deeply involved in promoting and developing the field. Private foundations, led by the C. S. Mott Foundation's $100 million investment in 21st Century Learning Centers and other major afterschool initiatives, are increasing their involvement at the program, policy, and research levels. The Mott Foundation and the U.S. Department of Education are working closely together to help develop a service, training, and evaluation infrastructure for the field. New projects are focused on promising practices, research databases, cross-city leaders' networks, community collaboration, and policy development, to name a few. Besides the many local foundations that support afterschool work, large national private foundations have been extremely supportive. The foundations include the Carnegie Corporation, Robert Wood Johnson Foundation, Wallace–Reader's Digest Funds, and many more. Perhaps not surprisingly, a whole industry of entrepreneurial afterschool educational services has arisen, offering everything from curricula units to educational enrichment programs. For those involved in education reform, afterschool programs can have a number of appealing characteristics: they are relatively cheap compared to reforming schools, they do not require major changes in institutional structure or practice, and they receive broad support from the American public.

Coordination of citywide responses

In urban centers across the country, the growth of an afterschool system has taken the field from discrete organizations running individual programs to collaborative citywide efforts aimed at providing children and youth with a seamless web of supports within their communities. Many cities have also developed a system of afterschool funding and integration, including New York City, where private philanthropic and municipal funding has resulted in approximately

$500 million over five years invested in collaborative programs, bringing community-based organizations, as well as cultural institutions and other partners into over 125 schools. Across the country, San Diego's 6 to 6 Extended Day Program expanded from $1.7 million in general funds in 1998 to a budget of over $17 million in 2002 from multiple funding sources. The result is programming in every elementary and middle school in San Diego. In Boston, the biggest public-private collaboration in the city's history has been established to strengthen the quantity and quality of afterschool time. Almost every major city in the United States now has some form of coordinated afterschool initiative.

These initiatives arise from different sources and take on various roles. Some are initiated by mayors and some by school superintendents, and others have an organization such as United Way as their catalyst. Nearly all aim to provide leadership, strategic development, and funds leveraging, and many also are involved with afterschool programs by providing technical and management assistance or contracting with afterschool program providers. For example, the Local Investment Corporation in Kansas City contracts with a variety of public and private providers to serve the city's students in over forty schools, and the After School Corporation oversees a model partnering community-based organizations and schools at over 125 sites in New York City and other locations in New York State. A number of city initiatives are led by private organizations that directly serve or contract with youth-serving organizations, such as BEST in Los Angeles, serving over thirteen thousand youth every year at seventy-eight sites, and community education departments in cities such as Denver and St. Louis.

Whatever their starting point, most initiatives follow a developmental pathway as they mature. Beginning with a process to create a vision with appropriate involvement from a wide variety of stakeholders, initiatives then often move onto assessments of resources, including those of youth themselves, and barriers to reaching their agreed-on vision. The first year or two of an initiative, unless it has begun with significant funding and a clear mandate, is a planning period, when assessments are conducted and a structure for the initiative itself is conducted. In many communities, there is no obvious home or hub for an initiative, resulting in either a search for an appropriate lead agency or tensions between competing organizations or departments. The new energy behind afterschool initiatives is derived from a wave of public support. Without such support, the initiative will not be able to develop needed momentum for implementation. Therefore, a great deal of energy during the planning phase must be invested in marketing the vision of the stakeholders and decisions of the leadership team.

Afterschools as sites of urban youth development

The growth of widespread afterschool programming in cities is not only associated with financial aid and social support. A new philosophy of collaboration is emerging, as youth and youth services are viewed through multiple perspectives at once, such as education, youth development, health, and safety. This philosophy is marked by an era of partnership, with institutions joining forces to address complex societal issues by finding common ground. Since September 11, 2001, the development of partnerships has gained new meaning. Whether it is the local YMCA that works with a school to serve children in the afterschool hours, a university connecting with a surrounding community, or a city convening funders and businesses, we seem to be moving beyond the so-called me or self era of the late twentieth century and into a time of shared social responsibility.

In the arena of youth development and afterschool education, we are witnessing a new ethos among funders, service providers, and community organizations as they join forces to create youth programs. The fact that afterschool programs are often constructed as collaborations makes them an especially interesting case in point of what is becoming a phenomenon in many sectors of society.

Intermediary afterschool spaces

Citywide initiatives are examples of large-scale collaborations that result in many diverse intermediary spaces for children. These spaces operate outside the structures of traditional institutions, even if they are located within them. For example, afterschool programs are frequently housed in schools, but are often in fact extensions of autonomous youth development organizations. Even organizations that single-handedly create afterschool programs are part of intermediary environments because they operate in communities and schools that are not under their control.

Furthermore, the program content may not be unified; it may represent diverse offerings from collaborating institutions and groups, such as homework, sports, arts, and recreational activities. Such flexibility may give rise to a lack of structure in many programs or a lack of integration with schools and the surrounding community, but the assets of this social space are enormous. We have found a number of common dimensions of intermediary spaces.[5] They are typically:

- Participatory and in a position to foster and model democratic ideals.
- In constant evolution and living in a realm of both productive tension between and nurturance from collaborating organizations.
- Creative and innovative; self-defined as different from traditional organizations.
- Vulnerable to potential power struggles as one collaborating group or another may vie for control.
- Models of leadership ideal and effective time use. They need to justify themselves by means other than efficiency.

What makes afterschool settings so fascinating is that as intermediary spaces, they are defined as much by what they are not as by what they are. Because they are not necessarily associated with the expectations of school or other major institutions, students may feel more at home in intermediary spaces. There is some evidence that afterschool programs can provide a much-needed link between the values, attitudes, and norms of students' cultural community and those of the culture of power.[6] (The culture of power refers to the beliefs and expectations transmitted by dominant social groups.) Delpit argues that school failure for many students is a result of inadequate access to the rules of the culture of power and lack of awareness on the part of those in the dominant culture of the existence and meaning of these power differences.[7] Heath coined the term *border zones* to describe effective youth programs.[8] In the more informal setting of an afterschool program, students may have the opportunity to connect with teachers and other adults as mentors who help them develop a sense of leadership and membership in this intermediary space.

Collaborations in cities around afterschool time

We have found these strengths and vulnerabilities not only in individual programs and their collaborative networks or in larger organizations working together to serve youth. Citywide efforts, the topic of this issue, are functioning under the same possibilities and constraints as well. City leaders cannot just force a citywide collaboration; they need to coax and cajole, convene and convince. Even with sufficient funding, which is rarely present, there is not one organization that can provide all the services youth need. Schools need to work together with a wide array of community-based organizations. Cultural institutions, sports clubs, clinics, and universities are typically part of the mix. It is this wealth of organizations, the coming together of different stakeholders, that makes this work so exciting. Organizations and their leaders are getting to know each other, and they are beginning to collaborate. More important, they are beginning to put intermediary structures in place that make such collaborations possible and sustainable. But it is also a fragile structure in most cities—one that could easily break down if not sufficiently nurtured by leaders, organizations, and funders.

The need for creative solutions in city programs

If afterschool programs are to begin to meet the many challenges inherent in today's increased expectations, they will need to be given the necessary resources with which to succeed. At a minimum, the field will need to foster a stable workforce, sustainable financing, and a knowledge base that creates the foundation for positive results.

Most afterschool staff are destined to be part-time staff, with the possible exception of those in administrative positions. Yet in order to meet the potential of afterschool programs, adults in the programs need a wide variety of skills and knowledge, from how to build students' literacy skills to an understanding of diverse cultures. While certified teachers may be the most appropriate staff for certain roles—helping older students with homework, for example, or providing additional academic learning time for small groups of children—they are unlikely to form the core workforce for afterschool programs as these programs expand. Yet if community-based agencies are to continue to provide the vast majority of afterschool programming, how will a part-time workforce create the kind of programs that will meet the goals of parents, educators, and voters?

This staffing paradox has yet to be solved, but hopeful experiments are under way. The Responsive Advocacy for Life and Learning in Youth (RALLY) program in Boston creates full-time jobs in middle schools for prevention practitioners, who work with at-risk students across their social and environmental contexts, both during the school day and in the afterschool program. Other programs are teaming up with museums and other youth-serving organizations to create joint staff positions for specialists who work at the museum during the day and in the afterschool program in the afternoon. A few schools are serving children in a seamless program from 8:00 A.M. to 5:00 P.M., hiring both credentialed and noncredentialed staff to work early and late shifts.

The sustainability challenge for these programs is also overwhelming. The assumption that local public funding will take the place of federal and state grants, over a one- to three-year time line, has little historical basis. While local school districts, counties, and municipalities are increasing their monetary and in-kind support for programs, they are unlikely to assume the full cost of programs, which research suggests runs between two and three thousand dollars per student per year for part-time programs and up to four thousand dollars per year for full-time (year-round) programs.[9]

Afterschool programs also face the challenge of successfully meeting the public's rising expectations. The newly formed Afterschool Alliance is promoting the field's expansion through a public awareness campaign, but such efforts will be short-lived without evidence of real changes for children and youth. As scaling up becomes the order of the day, we need much more information about what works, how, and for whom. We need to examine the ways in which active and informal learning environments can support not only enhanced cognitive outcomes but also the social and emotional competence so important to lifelong personal and professional success.

The pace of growth in the afterschool field over the past five years has been incredible, resulting in a panoply of investments at the local, state, and federal levels in the public and private sectors. We can now look to urban initiatives from coast to coast and in nearly every major city. However, states are now facing steep declines in budgetary resources, and afterschool initiatives are struggling to maintain their foothold in the public funding system. If we are to create urban environments that children and youth can use to discover their talents and passions, a united constituency will be needed to maintain these revolutionary spaces.

The following are a few suggested resources for those interested in doing further reading on this topic:

Association for Supervision and Curriculum Development. (2001). *Educational Leadership: Beyond Class Time, 58*(7).

Behrman, R. E. (Ed.). (1999). *The Future of Children: When School Is Out, 9*(2).

Clark, R. M. (1992, Summer). Why disadvantaged students succeed. *Connections*, 10–13.

McLaughlin, M. W. (1999). *Community counts: How youth organizations matter for youth.* Washington, DC: Public Education Network.

National Governors' Association. (1999). *Extra learning opportunities in the states.* Washington, DC: Author.

Noam, G. G., Biancarosa, G., & Dechausay, N. (2002). *Learning beyond school: Developing the field of afterschool education.* Harvard University. Available on-line: www.paerweb.org.

Posner, J. K., & Vandell, D. L. (1994). After-school activities and the development of low-income urban children: A longitudinal study. *Child Development, 35,* 868–879.

Additional suggested readings can be found on-line in the syllabus for the Harvard Graduate School of Education course: "The Afterschool Child: Development, Programming, and Policy" (http://www.gse.harvard.edu/~afterschool/H236.html).

Notes

1. Wilgoren, J. "The Bell Rings and the Students Stay." (2000, Jan. 24). *New York Times*, A:1.

2. We use the spelling *afterschool* because it conveys the institutional legitimacy of the field rather than a tangential add-on to the institution of school.

3. Afterschool Alliance. (2001, July–Aug.). *Afterschool alert poll report*. Available on-line: www.afterschoolalliance.org.

4. Seppenan, P. S., Love, J. M., deVries, D. K., Bernstein, L., Seligson, M., Marx, F., & Kisker, E. E. (1993). *National study of before and after school programs. Final report*. Portsmouth, NH: RMC Research Corporation.

5. Noam, G. G. (2001, May 10–11). Afterschool time: Toward a theory of collaborations. Paper presented at the Urban Seminar Series on Children's Mental Health and Safety: Out-of-School Time, Kennedy School of Government, Cambridge, MA.

6. Cooper, C. R., Denner, J., & Lopez, E. M. (1999). Cultural brokers: Helping Latino children on pathways toward success. *Future of Children, 9*, 51–57.

7. Delpit, L. (1995). *Other people's children: Cultural conflict in the classroom.* New York: New Press.

8. Heath, S. B. (1994). The project of learning from the inner-city youth perspective. In F. A. Villarruel (Ed.), *Promoting community-based programs for socialization and learning.* New Directions for Child Development, no. 63, 25–34.

9. Halpern, R. (1999). After-school programs for low income children: Promise and challenge. *Future of Children, 9*, 81–95.

GIL G. NOAM *is an associate professor of psychiatry/psychology at McLean Hospital and Harvard Medical School and associate professor of education at the Harvard Graduate School of Education, Cambridge, Massachusetts. He is the founding director of the Program in Afterschool Education and Research (PAER) at Harvard.*

BETH M. MILLER *is president of Miller-Midzik Research Associates and senior research adviser for the National Institute on Out-of-School Time in Wellesley, Massachusetts.*

SUSANNA BARRY *is manager of special projects for the Program in Afterschool Education and Research at the Harvard Graduate School of Education.*

The challenges that The After-School Corporation has faced in building and sustaining quality after-school programs that are accessible to every public school student in New York are discussed.

2

The long-term sustainability of after-school programs: The After-School Corporation's strategy

Lucy N. Friedman, Mary S. Bleiberg

WHEN THE *NEW YORK TIMES* 9/11 Neediest Fund awarded a grant to The After-School Corporation (TASC), the after-school movement in New York reached a significant benchmark. The generous grant of $2.6 million affirmed the value of after-school programs to the city's families and communities.[1] With this grant, TASC is creating and expanding quality school-based, after-school programs for about two thousand children at ten sites in Lower Manhattan. The new programs and services have been set up within three or four months, demonstrating that the infrastructure exists to establish after-school programs rapidly. In addition to helping children, parents, and staff cope with the continuing trauma and stress stemming from September 11, these programs will also provide academic enrichment, recreation, and arts in a safe, nurturing environment.

Special thanks to Mia Chung and Jeanne Mullgrav for their assistance with this chapter.

NEW DIRECTIONS FOR YOUTH DEVELOPMENT, NO. 94, SUMMER 2002 © WILEY PERIODICALS, INC.

The implementation of this grant has nonetheless posed a number of challenges for TASC and its mission of enhancing the quality, availability, and sustainability of in-school, after-school programs in New York City and State, and eventually across the nation. For the first time, TASC has a mandate to ensure that every public school in a discrete geographical area has an after-school program.

The grant and the issues that it has brought into immediate focus signify that TASC and the after-school movement in New York is maturing and gaining momentum. One could argue that the 9/11 Neediest grant is a dry run for TASC, raising many of the issues that it must grapple with if it is to reach its goal of making after-school available in every public school. The questions raised have touched the heart of TASC's mission and tested the resilience of its program model: Is the TASC program model flexible enough to accommodate all school communities? Recognizing that other quality after-school program models exist, will TASC alter how it defines its standards? Can the integrity of the model be maintained despite increasingly complicated (and constricting) funding requirements? Which government partnerships must still be developed to secure sustainable funding? What is the role of private funders as after-school transforms into a public responsibility?

Background and history of TASC

TASC's mission is to make high-quality after-school programs a public responsibility—financially sustainable and universally available to every public school student. TASC began in 1998 with a challenge grant from philanthropist George Soros's Open Society Institute (OSI) in response to changing social patterns. More and more parents juggle work and the demands of managing a single-parent household. In addition, welfare reforms, most notably the Personal Responsibility and Work Opportunity Reconciliation Act of 1996, ended federal entitlement to cash for needy families and required that all recipients of assistance seek employment. These social patterns have increased the need for child care and highlighted the lack of child care resources across all economic strata.

Growing programs, raising consciousness

OSI pledged up to $25 million each year for five years, contingent on three-to-one matching funds from the public sector and other private donors. TASC launched its activities in September 1998 with grants to twenty-five after-school programs in the five boroughs of New York City. Since then, the number of programs operating with TASC support has increased almost eightfold, serving children throughout New York City and in thirty counties in New York State. Currently, 207 TASC-supported programs are operating: 157 located in New York City and 50 spread around the state. The number of participants has grown concomitantly, from seven thousand to forty-nine thousand children.

With programs in 12 percent of New York City's public schools, TASC is having an impact on the city's consciousness. Principals at schools throughout the city are seeking support for after-school programs; TASC receives approximately four proposals for every grant available. In addition, Governor George Pataki and the New York State legislature have pledged to increase support for after-school programs. Based on TASC's progress to date and on the growing support nationally for after-school programs, OSI recently extended its initial five-year grant for two additional years. The 9/11 Neediest grant underlined the increasing prominence of after-school as a public good.

The TASC strategy

To achieve the goal of making quality school-based after-school programs a public responsibility, TASC's strategy is incremental growth. This growth is primarily determined by the rate of public fund development and could be accelerated through legislative action. TASC's strategy is multilayered:

Create a critical mass of effective programs that generate the public demand and political will needed to transform after-school into a universally available public institution.

Develop public and private partnerships for operation and funding of after-school programs.

Serve as an intermediary between programs, government, private funders, and business and cultural partners to facilitate program operations and advocate for public policies that sustain after-school programs.

Adopt a governance mechanism that is publicly accountable and preserves the integrity of the program model.

A critical mass of after-school programs

In collaboration with the New York City Board of Education and other New York State school systems, TASC supports after-school programs designed to enrich the lives of children and help their parents. TASC believes children should be exposed to a broad range of subjects and disciplines as part of their basic education. To be well educated in an information-rich society and to function responsibly, students need to know a great deal and to be able to think critically. After-school programs can play a strategic role in opening up children's minds and hearts to the challenges and rewards of formal learning by providing them with more time to absorb material and with opportunities to learn in different ways.

Building a program model

To develop a high-quality program model, TASC reviewed the wide variety of after-school programs in New York City and around the country. In particular, it looked at programs operated by Beacons, the Virtual Y, the Children's Aid Society, and settlement houses.[2] Taking important elements from each, TASC identified a core set of functional and staff requirements that work to create a model of a high-quality, affordable, and replicable after-school program.

Programs are based in public schools (grades K through 12) from 3:00 to 6:00 P.M., Monday through Friday, during the academic year. All students enrolled at a school with a TASC-supported program are eligible to attend the program, and daily attendance is expected. By having program enrollees attend every day, the programs can be varied, sophisticated, and responsive to the needs and interests of students, build community, and engage in projects and culminating events—and they are therefore more likely to have a significant and sustained impact on students' development and achievement.

On average, 30 percent of each school's attendees are enrolled in the after-school program—usually two hundred to four hundred children per program. By serving a significant portion of the school population, a program can have a qualitative, visible impact on the school. Principals, teachers, parents, and students are consequently more likely to become invested and supportive of it. Many programs include school-day teachers, aides, and paraprofessionals among their after-school staffs, which helps to create a consistent, extended-learning platform. The after-school program operated by the Police Athletic League at Public School (P.S.) 118, for instance, has the school's reading teacher on staff as the education coordinator; she assists the program in aligning its activities with New York City's academic performance standards. Similarly, California's Sacramento START after-school programs maintain alignment with the school day with the help of literacy coaches, who are also full-time teachers from the school sites.

Defining high quality

TASC's definition of high-quality after-school programs includes the following core elements:

Programming that provides homework help and enrichment activities, including literacy, science, math, arts, sports, community service, and field trips. In addition, TASC stresses health and social development (including drug prevention and nutrition). For high school students, programs include peer counseling, community service, internships, college preparation, and job training.

A supportive safe zone where children can make friends and relate comfortably to adults and where children from diverse cultures can learn about and respect their commonalities and differences.

Diverse staffing in a one-to-ten adult-student ratio that includes teachers, youth workers, artists, high school and college students, parents, and volunteers.

Parent involvement, from planning to implementation of activities.

Training and technical assistance for all staff.

Periodic evaluations of each program's effectiveness and adherence to core elements.

A full-time, year-round site coordinator.

Programs are operated by community-based organizations (CBOs), deriving strength from their community connections; the expectation is that these organizations will design programs in response to local needs, which often means accommodating multiple languages and cultures.

Varied programs and demonstrated effectiveness

Within these parameters, a range of effective program models and practices has been established. Currently, TASC-supported programs are operated by more than 130 different CBOs, ranging from small neighborhood groups such as the Carter G. Woodson Cultural Literacy Project in Bedford-Stuyvesant, to settlement houses such as East Side House Settlement in the South Bronx, to the affiliates of large national organizations such as the YMCA in Rochester.

The cost of these programs is approximately $1,500 per student per year. This figure largely represents operational costs, but it also incorporates the expenses of training, technical assistance, curriculum development, and evaluation, and the value of in-kind allocations, such as security, from the New York City Board of

Education. In addition, the U.S. Department of Agriculture provides a subsidy for snacks or supper equal in value to as much as $320 per student per year.[3]

After three years of operation, TASC's program model has begun to demonstrate its effectiveness. Principals report that parents are choosing schools based on whether they offer after-school programs. Because after-school site coordinators are often included on school leadership teams, their continuing presence helps stabilize the leadership of schools, particularly at schools with principal turnover. At two schools, the after-school programs were struggling to gain acceptance from the schools' teachers, who refused to share classroom space with the programs. When new principals took the helm at these schools, they encouraged the teachers to share space because they were familiar and comfortable with the TASC model from prior work at schools with TASC-supported after-school programs.

Building public and private partnerships

What makes the after-school movement at once so exciting and challenging is the complex universe of partnerships that it brings together. A diversity of federal, state, and local government agencies (agriculture, criminal justice, education, health, labor, and social service) funds programs operated by community-based and faith-based organizations, universities, and hospitals. These programs partner with all educational levels (from kindergarten to university), corporate leaders, unions, civic organizations, law enforcement, cultural organizations (such as museums), parents, and children.

TASC has built a number of partnerships that link public and private resources for both operation and funding of after-school programs. It brokers partnerships between CBOs that operate the programs and the schools that house them, between public and private funding sources and CBOs, and between training and technical assistance agencies and the programs. Each new partnership reflects a deepening public investment in providing quality after-school for all children.

Operations

TASC's collaborations with school systems and youth-serving agencies throughout the city and state form a strong foundation to transform quality after-school into a public responsibility in New York.

An essential component of the TASC model is its ability to leverage local resources in order to reduce the overall cost of its programs. By using school sites, TASC-supported programs extend the use of the public's tax investment in school buildings and also enable after-school activities to support and expand on school-day learning. In addition, locating programs in schools promotes the programs' accessibility. As more and more families, principals, teachers, and communities united in their investment in the importance of after-school programming, the initiative gains momentum.

A cornerstone of TASC's program model is operation of after-school programs by nonprofit CBOs.[4] CBO involvement helps to develop programs that are more responsive and reflective of the community than the school. CBOs and schools share many common goals, but their missions are different: whereas CBOs have the expertise and commitment to design educational activities, most are primarily dedicated to nurturing children's social and emotional development through enrichment activities. CBOs can support and expand on school-day learning by employing promising new educational and child development practices.

Perhaps most important, CBOs have strong ties to the communities they serve. Because CBOs often employ after-school instructors and counselors who live in the area and are familiar with its cultures, after-school programs can be crucial links between schools and families, particularly those that serve multilingual and recent immigrant communities. While schools can be intimidating to parents, CBOs seek to cultivate relaxing, informal, after-school environments and develop opportunities to involve parents in after-school activities, often as volunteers.

Critical to the growth and visibility of the TASC initiative is the ever-increasing network of partnerships with academic, cultural, and professional organizations to provide training and programming for after-school coordinators and staff. These relationships strengthen core academics, enhance arts and technological education, and develop career opportunities for participating youth. TASC relies on New York's Partnership for After-School Education (PASE), a citywide network of youth development professionals and community groups, for basic training of staff. TASC also contracts with a range of training partners, including the Democracy Project, the Harvard Graduate School of Education, the New York Foundation of Architecture, the Spaghetti Book Club, Studio in a School, the Whitney Museum, and many others.

TASC's partnership with the Madison Square Garden Cheering for Children Foundation (MSG), for example, provides after-school programs with a lively array of sports, arts, and literacy enrichment activities. Players and staff from the New York Knicks, Rangers, and Liberty and professionals from MSG Networks and Radio City Entertainment provide sports clinics and motivational presentations. MSG has also donated more than thirty thousand tickets for students and their families to attend sporting and entertainment events at the Garden and Radio City Music Hall.

Funding

The process of institutionalizing after-school programs in every public school requires visible and substantive support from both public and private spheres. Since each public funding partner brings the after-school initiative a step closer to its ultimate goal of after-school as a public responsibility, TASC aggressively taps public funds at the federal, state, and city levels.[5]

In FY 2002, public financial support for TASC increased to $52 million from $36 million in FY 2001. The percentage of public funding for FY 2002 is expected to increase to 70 percent up from 59 percent in FY 2001. At the federal level, TASC advocates to increase funding for the 21st Century Community Learning Centers. TASC also seeks to leverage federal child care subsidies and

Temporary Assistance for Needy Families funds—both important sources of sustainable funds. At the state level, TASC successfully supported the creation of New York's Advantage After-School program that helped create 120 after-school programs statewide. TASC also partners with the state's Extended Day/School Violence Prevention program. Both linkages represent important steps toward universal after-school in New York. TASC continues to work with the state to increase funds for the after-school movement.

For its city programs, TASC continues to advocate for increases in direct support from New York City. TASC's vital partnership with the board of education, which provides $8.5 million in matching funds to TASC-supported programs, provides a foundation for attaining universal after-school. The board's support includes various in-kind allocations, such as snacks, instructional supplies and materials, laptop computers, professional development, transportation of students with special needs, custodial fees, security, and fingerprinting. The board's allocation per student is approximately $230.

While TASC's goal is to raise the bulk of support for basic program operations from public funds, private support continues to play a vital role in a strategy of balanced growth. Private donations are expressions of taxpayers' desires—powerful demonstrations of how much individual citizens value and demand after-school programs. As such, private support serves as a powerful catalyst for public commitment. When the OSI launched TASC, it sparked a movement for after-school in New York; its vision garnered the public's attention, increasing awareness of the value of after-school and generating material support through an innovative relationship between public and private funds. By designing a challenge grant that requires matching funds on a three-to-one basis, OSI made the success of the after-school movement contingent on recognition and commitment by government and private funders. In some ways, the recent grant from the *New York Times* 9/11 Neediest Fund, which also requires matching funds, opens the next chapter on the funding of after-school: the grant is a significant vote for universal after-school programs, since all public schools in Lower Manhattan are targeted. Moreover, the grant may set a precedent for how TASC-supported programs, together with independent programs, may fulfill the objective of universal after-school.

Such private commitments convey a potent and influential message of how after-school programs are a significant vehicle not only to reform education but also to support communities. For corporate donors, supporting after-school can have a direct impact on the lives of their own employees, as well as being a long-term investment in society and the future workforce. As such, support from the private sector provides leverage for public funding. In addition, foundation grants are often more flexible about how funds are dispensed. They support core operations and advance key quality-enhancing initiatives. Moreover, private funds keep political leaders accountable to the public.

To date, TASC has received commitments of more than $15 million from corporations, foundations, and individuals. Increasing uncertainty about public funds, as well as the financial challenges facing many of TASC's CBO partners, makes the continuing support of private funders even more critical in coming years.

TASC's role as an intermediary

By serving as an intermediary among after-school programs, funders, and government and professional development agencies, TASC can help implement a cohesive and effective strategy for supporting and sustaining after-school programs in New York. TASC promotes efficiency and communication within the intricate web of partnerships that cradles after-school. As an intermediary, TASC operates as a broker and a buffer to facilitate the operations and funding of the programs it supports. It therefore must be responsive to many constituencies and balance a complex—and sometimes competing—assortment of needs and stipulations.

Operations and funding

Key partnerships with entities like the board of education and MSG are possible because TASC offers both efficiency and access: a single negotiation with TASC affects an expansive network of communities and institutions, as indicated by the *New York Times* 9/11 Neediest grant. Individual schools and CBOs may be less effective at seeking these partnerships and funds because they do not offer as wide a scope. For example, during spring 2000, TASC partnered with the New York City Board of Education's Office of Pupil Transportation; sharing costs and buses with other board of education extended-day programs, this pilot initiative transports students with special needs from three TASC-supported after-school programs to their homes.

TASC serves as a buffer between CBOs and funders, securing large sums from diverse funding streams that are then integrated and distributed to individual programs. This role is particularly significant for tapping a diversity of public funds. TASC leverages public dollars from various government silos—such as the New York City Human Resources Administration and the Department of Youth and Community Development—that in some cases individual CBOs would not be able to access. Government grants operate according to various funding models; some parcel out reimbursement child by child, and others are simple direct grants. TASC blends these funds for distribution to CBOs. Contract procedures are often cumbersome, so by relieving CBOs of the task of juggling multiple contracts with a variety of compliance stipulations, TASC enables them to focus on operating the after-school programs. And by taking on the responsibility of collecting and submitting data from sites, TASC relieves funders of the burden of multiyear grants management.

In addition, TASC acquires and maintains a large pool of funding, which safeguards against interruptions or shortfalls in cash flow to the CBOs, allowing programs to operate when grants are delayed in the bureaucratic maze. For the first three years, TASC's contract negotiations with city agencies extended for several months, and funds were not disbursed until May of each year; by this point in the academic calendar, after-school programs needed to have served ten months' worth of snacks and paid insurance premiums and salaries to teachers and staff.

TASC also facilitates the work of the after-school programs it sponsors through capacity building. By forming relationships with professional organizations such as the Lawyers Alliance New York,

TASC provides workshops for CBOs that strengthen their ability to operate all their services efficiently.[6] TASC has also built a network of providers that enable small CBOs to acquire operational necessities, such as insurance and workers' compensation, quickly. In addition, TASC bridges the communication between CBOs and government agencies by interpreting contract guidelines to make adherence to requirements less involved or helping individual CBOs acquire waivers when appropriate.

Advocacy

TASC represents numerous CBOs, schools, and agencies, advocating with a unified voice for the institutionalization of quality after-school programs. By demonstrating that the public values and demands after-school programs, TASC seeks to change public policies regarding youth development, education, and child care. It also collaborates with after-school initiatives in other jurisdictions to create and sustain a climate for public policy change.

TASC campaigns to increase funding for after-school programs overall. For the past three years, it has participated in Lobby Day for after-school in Albany as part of the Coalition for After-School Funding. In February 2002, the coalition organized over a thousand students, parents, teachers, and after-school staff members from across the state to seek increases in after-school funding; students went on escorted visits with legislators, which also served to educate students about how government works. TASC has also joined forces with the Afterschool Alliance, a national coalition of public, private, and nonprofit organizations dedicated to raising awareness of the importance of after-school, to advocate for quality, affordable after-school programs for all children by 2010.

Research and innovation

Bolstering its advocacy efforts, TASC works to broaden the base of information about what works in after-school programs through research, identification and dissemination of promising practices, and the publication of resource briefs on a variety of topics. Because TASC supports a significant number of programs, representing a wide variety of communities, it can undertake rigorous, intensive studies. Research demonstrating the benefits of after-school programs is crucial for increased public investment.

TASC has engaged Policy Studies Associates (PSA), a Washington, D.C.–based education policy research organization, to evaluate the effectiveness of the TASC initiative.[7] PSA is conducting an independent five-year evaluation to document program implementation, rates of student participation, and effects on participating organizations and the parents of after-school participants. The evaluation also identifies best practices and measures student outcomes, including student achievement, school attendance, and social development. TASC and PSA negotiated with the New York City Board of Education's Division of Assessment and Accountability to gather student performance data for schools hosting TASC-supported after-school programs and gained approval of data collection instruments, such as surveys and interview protocols.

Analyses and reports on TASC's first two years indicate promising trends and emerging issues that will be followed closely over the next three years. Overall, TASC-supported after-school programs established themselves as safe and inviting environments within their host schools and formed productive working partnerships with school principals, who facilitated the sharing of space and materials. Half or more of surveyed parents report that the programs fit their needs, allowed them to miss less work than before, and helped them keep their job and also work more hours. Forty-five percent of principals said that the after-school programs had increased parents' attendance at school events. Students reported feeling safe, relaxed, and happy at programs; they also felt that participating in after-school improves their social skills, including the ability to maintain self-control, make constructive choices about personal behavior, and avoid fights. Perhaps most noteworthy, school performance data show promising signs of increased school attendance and test scores for students who attended TASC-supported after-school programs regularly.

TASC's effort to identify and disseminate promising practices is a way to develop innovative educational practice. Programs serve as the research and development labs of the after-school field. To encourage the sharing of knowledge and promising practices among program sites and to recognize evidence of successful programming, TASC established a competitive award process with the support of the Citigroup Success Fund for Promising Practices in After-School Programs. TASC documents promising practices to share within the network of TASC-supported programs, as well as with the after-school community at large. For example, in 2000, the after-school staff at P.S. 123 (run by the New York University Metro Center for Urban Education) won an award for their method of snack distribution. With a system of snack monitors, snack distributors, and snack captains, the program developed a student-managed snack period that invested students with ownership of the program, promoted their leadership, and built a sense of community during the otherwise hectic period.

TASC also seeks to strengthen professional development in the after-school field. Recently, it teamed up with the City University of New York to launch Teach After Three, an initiative designed to help after-school staff members develop an educational and career plan to become full-time teachers. TASC believes that helping promising staff pursue teaching will improve the quality and staff retention of after-school programs; over the long term, Teach After Three aims to address the teacher shortage crisis in New York City.

Sustainability and quality management in the long term

As the number of after-school programs grows and the range of constituencies widens, TASC itself must evolve. The sustainability issues that TASC must grapple with include funding and accountability, standards and program model, and universality.

Funding and accountability

As the public responsibility for the financing of after-school programs increases, the question of how the after-school initiative is managed becomes more complicated. The decision regarding which funding streams to tap will have far-reaching ramifications for how TASC itself operates.

For a growing number of after-school programs, TASC must continue to maintain appropriate funding levels, manage diverse funding streams and in-kind contributions, and administer funds cost-effectively. Examples from around the country mirror TASC's experience that municipalities are the pivotal source for funding after-school programs in urban public schools. The advantage of local funding is that the political ties needed to sustain the funding are easier to maintain because positive results are visible; children can be seen actively and enjoyably engaged in learning rather than hanging out on the street. If, as appears to be the case, sustaining after-school necessitates great quantities of local funding, TASC must anticipate meeting increased standards of accountability to city government. As an entity that hopes to receive more than 90 percent of its funding from the public sector, TASC will have special responsibilities to taxpayers.

Another consideration for TASC will be the decision of whether to incorporate fees into its funding scheme. For many programs around the country, parent fees are the most significant source of revenue for after-school programs serving children from middle-income and affluent families; among programs that serve lower-income children, fees can sometimes be a component.

Standards and program model

As the number of programs grows, the after-school movement must grapple with how to maintain quality. If after-school programs are increasingly dependent on government funding and consequently increasingly subject to government regulation, TASC must evaluate the viability of its program model.

TASC's core elements were selected carefully to create a program model that is replicable, affordable, and adaptable to different settings, such as rural and urban communities. These core elements are also important institutional safeguards to develop after-school programs that are productive and appealing. TASC offers the programs it supports the freedom and support to explore and interpret the definition of quality. Integral to TASC's philosophy is the notion that several permutations of a quality program exist. While TASC requires that each program adhere to the core elements of the program model, it encourages each CBO and school to interpret these elements and design a program tailored to their students. TASC does not prescribe curricula, and each program varies according to the community it serves. The freedom to customize programs seems to be critical for CBO and school buy-in.

TASC is committed to advocating for and preserving the integrity of its program model. Nonetheless, it recognizes that other models of high-quality after-school programs exist; as exemplified by a commitment to research and evaluation, TASC will continue to investigate ways to improve and translate into practice its definition of a quality program.

As the after-school movement gathers momentum across the nation, it becomes increasingly important to consider whether an explicit concept of quality might be valuable and how to develop comprehensive program standards. Currently, TASC monitors the quality of the programs it supports by conducting appraisals and site visits, practices that may not be feasible as the number of programs grows. TASC is increasingly feeling the need to develop a formal set of standards that programs must meet. The challenge is that each TASC-supported program looks different; in addition, after-school programs across the nation offer different permutations of quality, a situation that is not necessarily amenable to a standardized system of evaluation.

Universality

Universality of appeal is one of the elements that will continue to have a significant impact on funding. From its inception, TASC has sought to meet the needs of a multitude of constituencies and an ever-widening diversity of program operators. By TASC's second year, each of the thirty-two school districts (K–8) in New York City had a TASC-supported after-school program.

Recently, while implementing the 9/11 Neediest grant, TASC faced several issues that complicate universal after-school. It confronted the sensitive issue of how free and fee-based programs can coexist at a few schools. And instead of its usual practice of fielding proposals from CBOs and schools for grants, TASC actively brokered partnerships between principals and CBOs to make sure that all schools in Lower Manhattan had a program.

TASC maintains its commitment to represent and serve a wide range of communities to demonstrate that after-school is a broad public need. Unsurprisingly, the largest portion of TASC-supported after-school programs are in the most economically challenged communities. However, middle-class communities are often powerful advocates and thus critical voices to assemble for the after-school movement. By representing a cross-section of New York's families, TASC can make the best case that after-school is an expression of the public will.

Looking ahead

In its first few years, the story of TASC has been that of a start-up movement—a rally to reform how schools and communities relate by tapping, connecting, and strengthening the resources currently available in neighborhoods and government. Distilling core elements from the best programs and research available at the time, TASC developed an after-school program model that is affordable and replicable in various settings. With the ultimate goal of making high-quality after-school programming accessible to all New York public school students, TASC continues to build a critical mass of quality after-school programs and widen a complex network of public and private partners.

As the after-school initiative matures, so must TASC's role evolve. Its efforts to nurture the expansion and visibility of after-school programs in New York have met with success thus far; after-school is increasingly developing an identity as a significant public good, demonstrating that it plays an important role in contributing to student achievement, helping parents, and strengthening schools. As government funding for programs increases, after-school makes steady progress toward becoming a public responsibility.

The after-school movement must negotiate the tension between quality and universality. Preserving quality while increasing the number of programs is a challenge. The accessibility of after-school programs is, in turn, dependent on the acquisition of adequate funds to establish and sustain programs. And the integrity of the program model must be reconciled with the increasingly labored stipulations of several funding sources.

As TASC looks to the future, it must weigh its core values, some of which may sometimes seem at odds with each other. In what ways will the TASC model be revised or loosened? How does TASC's vision of universality incorporate quality non-TASC programs? For communities without strong CBOs to partner with schools, what kind of support will CBOs need to operate quality programs? Will standards be effective in maintaining quality or simply create another layer in the bureaucracy of compliance requirements that after-school programs must navigate? Is a single-cost model advantageous for the after-school movement?

TASC's development of sustainable funding streams for after-school programs may also need to incorporate additional strategies—both traditional and innovative—as programs serve more varied communities. In affluent communities, for instance, charging fees may be the most expedient way to ensure that all children have access to an after-school program.

Like a protective parent, TASC must reflect on how to be most effective in helping the after-school movement achieve its potential. If after-school programs are eventually incorporated into public policy, TASC's role as broker, trainer, and fundraiser may not be expedient or even necessary. In time, the role of intermediary may give way to a primary responsibility of safeguarding quality. TASC may shift its role to concentrate on research and innovation of after-school practices. It can offer other communities guidance for nurturing after-school programs of their own and demonstrable strategies for bringing together a complexity of resources to improve the education of all children.

Notes

1. *The New York Times* 9/11 Neediest Fund awarded TASC a matching grant of $2.6 million to extend, expand, and create new school-based after-school programs in the vicinity of the World Trade Center site. The fund was initiated by The New York Times Company Foundation on September 12th. Donations from its readers had reached $60 million in March 2002. Of this amount nearly $20 million has been directed to job rescue, trauma treatment, legal assistance, and school support. Another $40 million has been dispersed through agencies in the field.

2. Beacons. Since 1991, community-based agencies have received core funding from the city to operate school-based community centers in eighty high-need neighborhoods. The centers are open after school and on weekends throughout the year, offering a range of youth development, educational and cultural programming to at least eighteen hundred different community residents annually, including adults. In 2002, TASC supported eleven after-school programs that were located in and integrated with Beacons.

The Virtual Y. The YMCA of Greater New York operates over ninety school-based after-school programs targeted to elementary school students in low-income neighborhoods. The programs average fifty students, have a 1:10 staffing ratio, and use enrichment curriculum developed for the Y.

Children's Aid Society operates nine community schools in NYC that offer students and their families a range of medical and social services in addition to after-school and evening programs 365 days a year.

New York City's thirty-six settlement houses have been providing after-school programming in community settings for generations. Some of the most important principles of youth development were developed in the organizations.

3. Snacks are valued at $80 per student per year. Suppers are valued at $2 per day, or as much as $320 per year.

4. Major government funds, such as the 21st Century Community Learning Centers, which were funneled through school districts, are now directly accessible by community-based organizations, supporting TASC's program model.

5. TASC receives support from several federal, state, and city sources, including the New York City Board of Education, New York City Council, New York City Department of Employment, New York City Department of Youth and Community Development, New York City Human Resources Administration, New York State Education Department, New York State Office of Children and Family Services, U.S. Department of Education's 21st Century Community Learning Centers, and the Corporation for National Service.

6. In addition to sheltering children when they might otherwise be involved in personally and socially destructive behavior, after-school programs arguably contribute to the overall well-being of communities. By building the capacity

of CBOs to operate efficiently, TASC is enabling CBOs to provide other services to their communities more effectively as well.

7. This evaluation is funded by the Charles Stewart Mott Foundation, the Carnegie Corporation of New York, and the William T. Grant Foundation.

LUCY N. FRIEDMAN *is president of The After-School Corporation.*

MARY S. BLEIBERG *is director of policy, planning, and fund development at TASC.*

Chicago has put in place a number of interwoven structures supporting young people during out-of-school hours, emphasizing alignment between community-based organizations and public entities.

3

Positive youth development initiatives in Chicago

Renae Ogletree, Tony Bell, Natasha K. Smith

WHAT IS CHICAGO doing to support young people when they are not in school? What are the gaps in services to meet the needs of students beyond school hours or youth who have dropped out? What is the city's strategy for youth development, and how does it address the need, individually and collectively, to improve programming? What does it take to build a web of supports for young people that help them develop across a range of outcomes?

The nation's current approach to the needs of young people is reactive, problem focused, fragmented, and incomplete. It may guarantee every youth a prison cell, but it cannot guarantee them an after-school program, job opportunity, or safe environment. Its programs fall short in quantity, quality, duration, and outreach to those most in need.

Out-of-school programming is a clear citywide priority. Chicago brings considerable resources to bear on the challenge of building a citywide infrastructure to support out-of-school programming, including commitments by Chicago Public Schools, the Chicago

NEW DIRECTIONS FOR YOUTH DEVELOPMENT, NO. 94, SUMMER 2002 © WILEY PERIODICALS, INC.

Park District, libraries, and other public delivery systems. Key elements of the strategy are coordination, collaboration, and alignment, especially between community-based organizations and public entities.

Need for change

Chicago's approach to youth development, *Blueprints for Change*, adopted in 1995 is based on the premise that all young people deserve opportunities and options during out-of-school hours.[1] Promoting consistent program standards among youth organizations and the professional development of those who work with young people are priorities of the *Blueprints for Change*, which include:

Building a strong and cohesive infrastructure for youth development, weaving together public and private, school and community, and family and agency resources in a comprehensive system of supports

Providing opportunities for all young people to participate in community and public life and to gain employment and leadership skills

Promoting policies and attitudes throughout the city and in every neighborhood that view young people not as problems to be fixed but as assets to be valued

Promoting youth development in a large urban center requires vision, sustained commitment, and decisive action. Chicago's out-of-school system is fortunate to have influential public leadership through the long-term commitment of Mayor Richard M. Daley and his wife, Maggie Daley, who have played a critical role in two of the most significant out-of-school initiatives: the citywide *Blueprints for Change* that led to the creation of the YouthNets (networks of youth development sites and services) and, more recently, the launch of After School Matters.

body," says Ray Vazquez, CDHS commissioner. "We believe the vision put forth by the Task Force remains valid and we are eager to take YouthNets to the next level. Funds freed up by switching from direct intervention to a strategy of prevention and youth development were reinvested in neighborhood delegate agencies, which could operate programs more efficiently and provide needed social support services for youth and their families."

More than two hundred delegate agencies, including private social service providers, neighborhood churches, watch groups, community coalitions, and businesses, participate in this citywide effort. In addition to funding and supporting direct programming for young people through this network of delegate agencies, the YSD supports coordination, quality standards, and professional development through YouthNets.

In partnership with a data research firm, CDHS conducted an assessment of the Chicago social services system. The study looks at poverty, youth development, early child care, homelessness, hunger, crisis response, and housing. Focus groups were held on each topic, and secondary research was reviewed. A 2002 report has been published.

According to CDHS, there are about 500,000 youth between the ages of six and eighteen in the city of Chicago. During out-of-school time, evenings, and weekends, the majority of programs and activities are provided by community-based youth agencies. The YSD provides funding to delegates to support services that are grounded in a youth development approach. By reinvesting in neighborhood delegate agencies, which operate programs within neighborhoods and provide much-needed social support services to children, youth, and their families, YSD is able to reach more children and youth. It is important to note that CDHS is one of the largest funders of youth development programs in Chicago.

In 2000, YSD administered more than $11 million to approximately 186 delegate agencies, which provided programming to thirty-nine thousand of the city's children and youth between the ages of six and eighteen. For the most part, programming takes place year round during out-of-school time in areas such as after-school activities, mentoring, counseling, and special events. It also oversees training, program standards, and youth worker certification.

In addition to CDHS, numerous other city agencies provide youth programming, including the Department of Cultural Affairs, the Mayor's Office of Workforce Development, the Mayor's Office for People with Disabilities, the Chicago Police Department through the Chicago Alternative Policing Strategy, the Department of Public Health, the Office of Violence Prevention, and the City of Chicago Commission on Human Relations.

Chicago Youth Agency Partnership

The Chicago Youth Agency Partnership (CYAP), established in 1994, is a nonprofit collaborative organization of forty youth-serving organizations and academic institutions. CYAP provides technical assistance and training to these organizations that want to embrace a positive youth development approach and professional development to increase the pool of skilled, knowledgeable youth workers. It also increases the capacity of organizations to develop new programs, policies, and resources that result in better outcomes for youth and creates standards and identifies best practices to which youth workers should aspire. CYAP offers a range of training options, including a thirty-two-hour intensive Advancing Youth Development Training Curriculum that introduces youth workers to a youth development approach to youth work, as well other competency-based topics. Since its inception, CYAP has trained over seven hundred youth workers. Participants have included youth service organizations, congregational youth ministers, Chicago Public School outreach workers, juvenile detention workers, YouthNets staff, and Aurora University degree-seeking students.

In 2001, CYAP trained 123 youth workers in its Advancing Youth Development Curriculum, and over one hundred received other competency-based training. CYAP receives funding from a diverse pool of public and private sources. Recently, it was the recipient of a three-year grant from the National Building Exemplary Systems for Training Youth Workers Initiative, funded by the Wallace–Reader's Digest Funds, that seeks to expand youth worker training programs and build networks of local youth-serving organizations in order to share resources, identify strategies, and build capacities of youth workers. CYAP is taking part in a national evaluation on the effects of training on youth workers. Most recently, it was awarded funding from the U.S. Department of Labor to implement a youth worker practitioner program with Chicagoland Youth Workers.

Chicago MOST

In 1994, the Wallace–Reader's Digest Funds and the National Institute for Out-of-School Time launched the Making the Most of Out-of-School Time (MOST) Initiative in Seattle, Boston, and Chicago. MOST was designed to respond to the increasing and changing demands for and on after-school and out-of-school programs. These changes, due in part to shifts in the economy, increased participation of women in the workforce, and weakened community infrastructure, were particularly devastating to communities already hit by poverty and few resources.

In 1995, Chicago MOST received a three-year grant of $1.2 million. This was followed by $750,000 in 1998 to extend its efforts to develop a communitywide system for providing before- and after-school care for those five to fourteen years old and to share lessons from this work with other cities. The goal of this citywide initiative is to increase the quality and quantity of before- and after-school care. Because MOST believes this can best be accomplished through collaboration among public and private partners, it operates as an intermediary. The major partners in Chicago are the Chicago Park District, the Chicago Community Trust, the Day Care Action Council, and the Chicago Department of Human Services. Chicago MOST has used three strategies to reach its goal:

Program improvement: Increasing the number of out-of school-time programs, providing training through various collaborations to enhance program activities, and supporting and offering resources to improve program facilities

Staff development: Connecting directors of community-based organizations to resources and technical assistance to improve their programming, helping to create relevant college courses and providing tuition reimbursement, and sustained involvement with professional development committees to address concerns about quality after-school programs

Partnership and system-building activities: Strengthening programs' relationships with resource and referral agencies to make sure that information is being disseminated to parents and other providers, working with the Chicago Park District to improve the Park Kids Program and providing funding for educational programs at organizations such as the ETA Theatre and Chicago Children's Museum to allow additional children to participate, and building a relationship with the Mayor's Office to promote leveraging of public funds and coordination of children and youth programs

Children, Youth and Families Initiative

In 1990, the CCT, in an effort to focus the city's attention on the needs of children and families, commissioned the Chapin Hall Center for Children at the University of Chicago to assess the history and current state of services to children and families and offer recommendations for improving that system. After an in-depth study, Chapin Hall proposed an alternative model for the delivery of social services—a comprehensive system that would integrate both primary and specialized services. Chapin Hall defined primary services as the broad array of programs and activities that are available to young people and their families every day, which have no special criteria for participation and no minimal costs associated with them, unlike specialized services for which young people are assessed only once a problem has been identified. Also integral to this alternative service delivery model was that it be community based, in acknowledgment of the legitimacy and expertise of communities in identifying their own needs and designing responsive programming to engage children and their families.

In 1991, the CCT launched the Children, Youth and Families Initiative (CYFI) to explore the feasibility of this alternative model. CCT committed $30 million over ten years to seven communities spread across the city, fairly representative of the conditions faced by moderate- and low-income children and their families in Chicago: Grand Boulevard, Logan Square, North Town, North Lawndale, Southwest, Uptown-Edgewater, and West Town.

A major goal of the initiative was to promote the healthy development of children, youth, and families by increasing the quantity and quality of primary supports available in communities. Each community proceeded differently in fulfilling this mandate, yet all made significant contributions to increasing the number of primary supports. In some communities, due to rapid demographic shifts and disinvestments, very little social service infrastructure remained, and what infrastructure existed was unresponsive to current community needs. As a result, the efforts of stakeholders, supported by the CYFI, made a huge difference in providing much-needed after-school and out-of-school activities. According to the report by Chapin Hall, during the first six years of the initiative, "75 percent of the Trust funding supported the creation of expansion of twenty-nine primary service programs involving over 200 organizations."[3] According to the report, thousands of young people participated in programming that allowed them to develop their untapped leadership skills, build their athletic prowess, expand their interest in science, or explore parts of the city they are unfamiliar with and develop a broader sense of community. Communities were able to collaborate at the local level, fulfilling another goal of the initiative. Stakeholders pooled their experience and resources to provide better and more expanded programs than any one individual provider could have offered. Chapin Hall reported that twenty-one thousand children and youth were served during 1997 alone. Recognizing the broader importance of this effort, the communities came together and hosted several citywide events.

As the ten-year commitment is drawing to a close, CYFI stands as an important citywide response, the impact of which has yet to be fully assessed. From a basic sustainability perspective, all of the collaboratives are still active and important community institutions, having diversified their funding streams and solidified community roles for participating programs. Within the past two years, the directors of the seven collaboratives have begun to meet with several important goals in mind: to sustain the cohesion of the seven communities; continue to build relationships with city, county, and state officials in an effort to continue the dialogue about social service reform; and seek additional funding to further the goals of the initiative, particularly the goal of quality service provision to children, youth, and families across the city.

After School Matters

After School Matters, a newly designed initiative of the City of Chicago, aims to build on the existing infrastructure of schools, parks, and libraries in a way that engages the interests of young people (older youth in particular), provides extracurricular activities, and creates job training opportunities that can lead to employment. Supported heavily by Maggie Daley and Chicago's Office of Human Infrastructure, the city has received a grant from the Robert Wood Johnson Foundation for $5 million to support the program over five years, in addition to other private and corporate support.

Currently, twelve Chicago public high schools, parks, and libraries are involved in the initiative. During this pilot phase, the goal is to involve at least five thousand students ages fourteen through eighteen, engage eighteen hundred students in employment and the others in community service projects, and demonstrate best practices and define program standards for engaging youth in after-school programs. In Chicago's Englewood community, where poverty and crime rates are prevalent, After School Matters flourishes at Robeson High School. The hope is that by 2005, at least 50 percent of the city's youth will participate, eventually involving children as young as ten years old.

There are three components to the program, with goals to increase young people's exposure to the arts, technology, and sports in a way that expands experience leading to actual employment. Gallery 37 provides young people with education and on-the-job training in the visual, literary, media, culinary, and performing arts. Gallery 37 began with 250 youth in 1991 in an effort to enliven a vacant plot of land known as Block 37. Over nine years, it engaged about twenty thousand high school students between the ages of fourteen and eighteen. Professional artists mentor the young people, who participate, cultivate art and life skills, and provide career mentorship. Gallery 37 employs more than four thousand apprentice artists between the ages of fourteen and twenty-one, who teach the arts to other children and youth between the ages of ten and twenty-one in downtown locations, public schools, parks, and community centers across the city. In addition to teaching, the apprentice artists produce their own art for public installation, performance, publication, and sale at the Gallery 37 Store.

Tech 37 recruits youth interested in technology to work with high-tech corporations and develop marketable computer skills. Students are exposed to a range of technology experiences and careers through a curriculum designed in conjunction with local corporations and other partners. In summer 2001, paid internships at local technology companies were available for one hundred youth. A technology incubator was developed where the most advanced students worked with technology professionals on state-of-the-art projects.

Sports 37 was designed to increase opportunities for youth to get involved in sports by expanding and better coordinating programs that currently exist in schools, parks, and CBOs. This initiative will create new sports and fitness opportunities for over four thousand youth. Students will also be able to earn service points by assisting coaches and team mangers or by being involved in a range of fitness programs; these points will be redeemable for incentives that include admission to sporting events, health clubs, and museums. As with the other components of After School Matters, youth will have opportunities to use the skills they have learned in ways that will lead to paid employment. For example, After School Matters participants would be eligible for the two hundred youth sports counselor positions that the Park District is piloting in summer 2002.

YouthNets

In June 1993, in response to increasing youth violence across the country, including Chicago, Mayor Daley established the Youth Development Task Force, consisting of public and private agency representatives, youth, civic leaders, university faculty, parents, and community members. The goal of the task force was to identify the challenges that face Chicago's young people and develop strategies for improving their lives. The task force presented its findings and recommendations in its June 1994 report, *Blueprints for Change.* The task force outlined five major challenges confronting youth and recommended that the city adopt a new mission: to improve the lives of Chicago's young people by embracing a positive youth development approach to meeting their needs and building their competencies. Chicago YouthNets was proposed as one programmatic strategy to meet these challenges.

Founded on many of the same underpinnings as CYFI, the city initiated Chicago YouthNets, intended to be a web of supports that extend from the family outward into the community. These networks of youth development sites were to be community based and supported by all levels of government. They were to provide young people and their families with a safe haven, access to services, engaging activities, and chances to build relationships and discover new opportunities. This design was predicated on the belief that the healthy development of young people occurred when programs and services are derived from a positive youth development orientation and connected to a cohesive infrastructure within the communities and ultimately across the city. These programs were to provide services to children ages six through eighteen between the hours of 2:00 P.M. and 6:00 P.M.

"Our first consortium meeting had a big turn-out. I think other agencies in the community were curious because traditionally our groups were competing—for youth, recognition and grant money," said Christopher Mallette, Sixth District YouthNet director. "That meeting put people at ease and we are already working together. Several agencies that were planning to submit applications for the After School Matters Sports 37 Grants are now combining their requests. As a district pulling together, I think we have a better chance of getting more money."

"Some people were skeptical at first about the YouthNets not providing direct services," continued Mallette. "But there are limits on how many youth we can serve at one time. By reaching out to the community we can get more youth involved and offer a wider variety of programming. We really are going to serve more young people this way. Isn't that what matters most?"

In 1994, six sites were selected: the Wentworth, Pullman, Wood, Austin, Foster, and Prairie districts. Many of these sites overlapped with the CYFI communities, and as with CYFI, the YouthNets sites that were selected reflected the diversity of Chicago's twenty-five police districts in terms of population, racial and ethnic composition, and socioeconomic conditions. In each district, it was left to the local stakeholders to determine how best to structure their YouthNet to meet the needs of children and youth and reach the goals outlined in *Blueprints for Change*. In some districts, the activities took place at a park district facility or a school; in others, supports were provided through one main location with several satellites sites throughout the community and included the broad array of primary supports that contribute to the healthy development of children and youth.

CDHS funded twenty-four YouthNets in 2001 located in twenty-four of twenty-five police districts, with the expectation that ten thousand youth and their families will be provided with a wide array of opportunities and positive activities. Each site is expected to recruit and retain a minimum of 150 youth (primarily fourteen to eighteen years old). In addition to this programmatic responsibility, the coordination and networking role of YouthNets was reaffirmed through an internal review. YouthNets are expected to act as catalysts, bringing together youth, local public and private agencies, and other community stakeholders, such as Chicago Alternative Policing Strategy, local public and private schools, parks, libraries, neighborhood-based service providers, other CDHS delegate agencies, faith-based institutions, and businesses and community members to form a partnership that will meet the increasing need for quality programming during out-of-school time. These partners will remain involved in all phases of the initiative: planning, implementation, and evaluation. Sites will be selected through a request for proposal process; those selected will receive $145,000 to $160,000 for a two-year period. Second-year funding will be contingent on the grantee's meeting its goals and objectives and on the availability of funding. The YSD had outlined four areas in which it expects the YouthNet sites to be able to demonstrate concrete outcomes: community planning and partnership; youth involvement; outreach; and enhanced program options, access, quality, and education.

YouthNets played a dynamic role in the community during 2001 in the areas of youth involvement, integrated services, and program quality. Under the new model, the programs included these enhancements:

YouthNets are now seen as a one-stop resource center. Youth can visit with staff to talk about their interests and needs, have available options presented to them, and get help enrolling on-site in the programs of their choice.

Each YouthNet now has an active Youth Council organized with a peer outreach worker (a youth) charged with the mission to discuss issues, advise on the Youth Outreach Action Plan, organize youth-sponsored events, and intensify efforts to get more youth involved in structured out-of-school activities.

Fifty Youth Council members are trained, evaluated, and recommended for funding over fifty summer program proposals developed and submitted by young people for CDHS Youth Empowerment grants.

Each YouthNet houses College View, an interactive computer program that supports educational goals by providing virtual tours of colleges and universities across the country for high-school-age youth and their parents.

Outreach coordinators have been hired at each YouthNet to develop an intensive strategy to engage youth ages fourteen through eighteen who have not previously participated in structured programs. These efforts also include a renewed relationship with the Chicago Public Schools Outreach Worker Program to facilitate linkages among community organizations and take steps to connect young people with activities.

Through the reorganization of the consortium, YouthNets have developed community networks to build a strong and cohesive referral infrastructure that connects young people with community resources.

Community stakeholders who agree to accept referrals of additional youth from the YouthNets now have access to a pool of YouthNet funding dollars to enhance and provide additional support for programming and special events it sponsors.

"Our outreach coordinator and Jillian Stillwell, our peer outreach worker, have developed a plan to saturate the area with information about the YouthNet," said Mallette. "They have organized mini-assemblies at schools and will hit the streets in April 2002, visiting parks, clubs and even corners to reach out to youth in our community."

In summer 2001, YouthNets hosted Youthology 2001. Conceived, planned, and implemented by youth, this day-long event brought five hundred young people together at Malcolm X College. They met with college representatives, learned about job and career opportunities, and attended workshops that ranged in subject matter from community planning to celebrating diversity.

The outcomes of the YouthNets initiative include:

More opportunities for young people to become involved in constructive and engaging activities

More young people making positive life choices and becoming engaged in positive, rewarding activities

More young people who see themselves—and are seen by others—as capable and valued resources

A chance for young people in all Chicago neighborhoods to grow up in a physically and psychologically healthy environment

A generation that is educated, skilled, and ready to enter productive adulthood

YouthNet Demonstration Project: Rogers Park YouthNet, Twenty-Fourth District

Rogers Park is located about ten miles north of downtown Chicago in the far northeast corner of the city, bordering Evanston. It is known as one of the most culturally and economically diverse neighborhoods in Chicago, with more than eighty languages spoken among the community's sixty-four thousand residents. Youth under age eighteen make up 24 percent of the total population; 28 percent are Hispanic, 30 percent African American, and 31 percent Caucasian. Keeping crime and victimization rates low is a concern of the residents of Rogers Park.

The 1998 Chicago Police Department annual report places the Twenty-Fourth District as virtually tied for fourth place for least amount of reported crime among the districts. A significant number of community members, including youth, are concerned about criminal activity, particularly relating to drugs and gangs. Increasing concerns also revolve around the lack of quality programming for youth ages fourteen to eighteen and a disparity in funding from the Chicago Park District.

Process

In 1997, the City of Chicago released a report calling for coordination among community agencies for the benefit of all children. The Rogers Park Community Council surveyed 550 community youth and inventoried neighborhood resources. The research found only limited programs available for youth fourteen through eighteen years old.

Now, as the Rogers Park YouthNet—Twenty-Fourth District approaches its fourth year, it has grown to be the leading community coordinator. It focuses on the four key components of Youth-Nets: community planning and partnership; youth involvement; outreach and enhanced programs; and access, quality, and evaluations. It works through many arenas in its role as a community clearinghouse: the Police Department, public library, park districts, public and private schools, community-based organizations, faith-based institutions, and other public and private institutions throughout the community and city.

Activities

The Rogers Park YouthNet has initiated a number of activities aimed at coordination of services and meaningful youth involvement.

Rogers Park Consortium. Working with approximately eighty organizations, the YouthNet has organized a community consortium that meets monthly. With the input of a wide range of organizations, the Rogers Park Consortium has developed a mission statement that promotes a holistic approach to serving youth in the community. Currently, the consortium is developing and implementing a community action plan to assess and fully serve the needs of youth in the community. This action plan includes surveying youth services providers about school and after-school services and surveying youth to identify the types of services they need in order to develop responsive programming.

As the coordinating body in developing the consortium, the YouthNet worked hard at gaining the trust of participants and keeping issues focused on youth and their needs. The process of developing initial trust depended on fostering a cooperative relationship. The YouthNet hosted events that allowed agencies to highlight their programs and activities and worked hard to engage youth in those events. This laid the groundwork for system building on issues relating to youth. As the relationships progressed, the YouthNet began to coordinate activities with partner agencies. This developed deeper relationships that brought agencies together in the organizational and planning stages.

The final stage that the Rogers Park YouthNet—Twenty-Fourth District is moving toward is true collaboration, so that the Rogers Park Consortium will be seen as an alliance of community-based organizations, schools, parks, libraries, faith-based institutions, parents, youth, and residents working as a unified entity in support of youth.

Youth Involvement. The most rewarding component of the YouthNet has been the involvement of youth. The YouthNet has worked hard at keeping youth at the forefront of all decision making.

Eighteen-year-old Jamelle Ward stood in front of a room full of police officers. He was not in any kind of trouble or completing community service hours required for school. He was speaking to the Twenty-Fourth District Advisory Committee, made up of local police, on behalf of the Rogers Park YouthNet. "I never thought I wanted to be anywhere near the police," said Jamelle. "I figured that if I stayed out of trouble they would mind their business and I would mind mine. But now that I go to these meetings I am learning how we can work together. The officers I meet really listen to me and now I can see where they are coming from." Jamelle was able to convince the committee to sponsor fifteen youth from the YouthNet to attend an overnight Teen Violence Prevention Retreat downstate.

The youth governing body, the Youth Council, consists of ten to fifteen teenagers, ages fourteen through eighteen, led by teen peer outreach workers and advised by the outreach coordinator. The Youth Council has been active throughout the year, attending leadership trainings, planning youth special events, participating in Community Alternative Policing Strategies (CAPS) Beat Meetings, as well as District Advisory Committee meetings. Youth Council members and the peer outreach workers have been responsible for recruiting teenagers to participate in the newly created high school fraternity and sorority and citywide Youth Expo, with workshops designed and facilitated by teenagers. In addition, youth from the council were responsible for the design and presentation of a youth-led workshop for parents, "How to Talk to a Teenager? Straight from the Source," which was presented at six of Mayor

Daley's citywide Parent/Neighborhood Assemblies. This gave the teenagers an opportunity to share with parents effective methods of communication between parents and teens.

Readiness for change

The need for community collaboration is also necessary for improved service delivery within neighborhoods.[4] Identifying assets and addressing gaps within a community can help determine what needs to be done to improve service delivery and how to build on what already works. The need for an entity to serve as community coordinator is also necessary to bring all stakeholders to the table to focus on one common goal and systematically address and identify a plan to improve conditions. In addition, young people need to be involved in the process of community building, with opportunities to participate and have meaningful roles in their community. Adults must develop young people by empowering them with the necessary tools to take charge of their futures.

The standards and expectations outlined by the mayor's *Blueprints for Change* and the Chicago Department of Human Services/Youth Service Division raised the bar for children and youth programming in Chicago for all of the stakeholders—community members, local service providers, and city government—and were met to varying degrees. At the very least, the YouthNets provided a new supply of after-school and out-of-school-time programming to meet the increasing city need, and at the most, it set standards for youth service provision that should challenge all youth providers.

Challenges and learning experiences

This chapter provides only a glimpse into how to provide access to and use schools during students' out-of-school time and what programs and initiatives fill out-of-school hours in Chicago. It also highlights themes in need of further exploration as the dialogue about out-of-school time continues in Chicago:

More effective coordination between the key players and partners, including identifying who the key partners are. Chicago still has a long way to go before all of its youth are engaged. In order to respond to this need and create an alternative social service delivery system that engages 100 percent of youth, Chicago will need to coordinate efforts of the city, state, and federal government (all relevant agencies and departments); the philanthropic community; the nonprofit sector; education; the business sector; and communities across the city. While this will not be an easy task, both the CYFI and YouthNets offer lessons on engaging a wide array of stakeholders and building some of the necessary elements of this infrastructure. If Chicago is going to be successful in this effort, a comprehensive plan that moves well beyond the previous initiatives will be needed.

For the most part, these efforts do not reach the hardest-to-serve youth in communities: youth with disabilities, school dropouts, drug-addicted youth, youth who are questioning their sexuality, gang-involved youth, and others. These young people receive less than their share of resources and effort.

We need to develop better ways to track who is and who is not being served and what is needed in order to engage and serve them effectively. As an out-of-school agenda for Chicago is being set, we must rigorously track which young people are systematically being missed and develop a concrete plan to engage them.

As we continue to think about the resources necessary to support the ever-increasing need for out-of-school programming for all of Chicago's young people, there are several questions that we will need to answer:

• What are the relationships between a variety of stakeholders so that schools can be accessed after hours?

- How do we evaluate the program? What works well, best, where, and when?
- Should activities be held in community-based locations or schools?
- How is out-of-school programming being funded, and what are the various sources of funding? Given an analysis of those data, what will be the funding needs in the future? What type of funding mix will be required to support future out-of-school needs?

Next steps

Each of the initiatives explored here coexists in a new infrastructure of initiatives with the continued focus on enhancing and building an even more cohesive web of supports during the out-of-school hours on a daily basis:

Standards: CDHS Youth Services Division will be involving a broad range of stakeholders in the process of creating standards for programming in the out-of-school hours.

Policy: Two efforts aim to move a policy agenda around out-of-school time. First is a working group, including representatives from the Day Care Action Council, Chicago MOST, CDHS Youth Services, Illinois Department of Human Services, Chicago Public Schools, Chicago Park District, and community-based organizations, charged with forging a public policy agenda. In addition, legislation has been submitted to the Illinois legislature to increase support for after-school programming.

Professional development and certification: CDHS Youth Services Division has convened a range of stakeholders to discuss issues of professional development and youth worker certification.

Program gaps: Increased attention is being paid to schools on a vision for out-of-school-time programs. The inception of After School Matters, which is currently receiving the greatest attention, builds on and reflects existing community infrastructures.

Outreach: After some years of focus on service provision and programming, YouthNets have returned to their original commitment to neighborhood-based coordination. This reorientation involves efforts to assess supports and needs in these neighborhoods, in addition to new opportunities for collaboration and alignment.

Funding: After School Matters generates private resources that can be used for program enhancement.

Advice for other cities

Cities that have demonstrated an interest in improving programming in the out-of-school hours must engage in a process of dialogue, planning, and public and private funding partnerships to create a policy and developmental framework of sustainability that will increase the number of quality programs available to all children and youth. This engagement encompasses the following process:

1. Intelligence gathering. Begin by mapping the existing resources and programs and initiating an effort to develop a comprehensive and coordinated approach to out-of-school time.
2. Promoting partnerships. Ensure that the city infrastructure is willing to partner with one or more key players in youth development to implement the project consistent with locally defined needs and to forge a shared vision of after-school challenges and opportunities.
3. Building public will. Focus on and mobilize a sustained municipal role in the development of a local after-school system over time that must include youth involvement.
4. Documentation and follow-up. Use the experience to refine the policy development framework and synthesize recommendations to improve programming in the out-of-school hours.

Notes

1. Mayor's Youth Development Task Force. (1993). *Blueprints for change.* Chicago: Author.
2. Chicago Department of Human Services, Forum for Youth Investment. (2001, June). *Progress and possibility: In the out of school hours, a status report.* Chicago: Author.
3. Chicago Department of Human Services. (2001).
4. Morrison, J. D., Howard, J., Johnson, C., Navarro, F. J., Plachetka, B., & Bell, T. (1997). Strengthening neighborhoods by developing community networks. *Social Work, 42*(5), 527–534.

RENAE OGLETREE *is director of the Youth Services Division in the Chicago Department of Human Services.*

TONY BELL *is coordinator for Mayor Daley's YouthNet initiative in the Chicago Department of Human Services, Youth Services Division.*

NATASHA K. SMITH *is Twenty-Fourth Police District YouthNet director at the Rogers Park Community Council, Chicago.*

Boston's efforts to expand after-school programs and build their capacity to support the standards-based education reforms of the city's public schools are explored.

4

Schools alone are not enough: After-school programs and education reform in Boston

Jennifer Davis, David A. Farbman

SINCE THE RELEASE of *A Nation at Risk* in 1983, the public has rallied around the educational mission of imparting to the next generation of Americans the high level of skills and knowledge needed to compete in the ever-intensifying global marketplace.[1] In consideration of the reality that children spend only 20 percent of their waking hours in schools (based on a 180-day school year and 6.5 hours of school of a typical day, with 14 waking hours), however, the prospects for success are uncertain at best. The standards reform movement has taken monumental, if erratic, steps in raising both the expectations for students and the schools' capacity to reach these expectations, yet ultimately, the impact of the standards movement may be limited by the most basic of elements: time. Without adequate time within the traditional school day and year

We thank Kathleen Traphagen, executive director of the Boston 2:00-to-6:00 After-School Initiative, and Beth Langan, of Parents United for Child Care, for their valuable comments throughout the writing of this chapter.

NEW DIRECTIONS FOR YOUTH DEVELOPMENT, NO. 94, SUMMER 2002 © WILEY PERIODICALS, INC.

to help all students reach these standards, the ultimate goal may prove elusive. As the Massachusetts Commission on Time and Learning averred in its 1995 report, "It has become increasingly obvious that campaigns for higher standards of learning on the one hand and for sufficient time to achieve those standards on the other are wholly interdependent. They stand or fall together."[2]

A growing body of research shows that participation in after-school and summer programs—whether they are activity focused, narrow tutoring sessions, or some combination—can help raise grades and scores on standardized tests and encourage positive attitudes toward school and learning.[3] An emergent cadre of educators and policymakers has begun to beat the drums of after-school programs as integral to the success of the education reform movement. Boston is one of the places where this drumbeat is being heard, and as a result, the education establishment and the work of after-school programs are moving closer together in their goals and practices.

In order to evaluate the role of after-school programming in the context of Boston's school reform efforts, we will describe in broad strokes the main characters of the story: the Boston Public Schools (BPS), the mayor and other key civic leaders, and the landscape of after-school programming in Boston. We will also examine more closely some of the key accomplishments of the central office charged with aligning the work of after-school programs and BPS, the Boston 2:00-to-6:00 After-School Initiative. This story highlights both the incremental nature of this undertaking on a systemic level and the wide variety of challenges that this undertaking has presented. As part of this story, we will look at two major efforts to move the after-school field closer to the schools: the Mayor's Task Force on After-School Time and the After-School for All Partnership. Finally, we will review a pilot project that grew out of the mayor's task force to describe how the endeavor to meld the goals of BPS reforms with after-school programs is playing out at particular Boston sites.

History and background

In 1995, based on the strong recommendation of Mayor Thomas M. Menino, the Boston School Committee hired Thomas Payzant as superintendent of schools. Payzant, the former superintendent of San Diego Unified District, brought with him a national reputation as an even-handed reformer who was more inclined to generate consensus than conflict. He had also played a national role in promoting the standards movement, and Menino thus made clear his own personal commitment to raising the academic standards of the Boston Public Schools.

Reforming the Boston Public Schools

Taking the reins in October 1995 (after a two-year stint as the assistant secretary for elementary and secondary education with the U.S. Department of Education under Richard Riley), Payzant promised to bring substantial reform to Boston's struggling schools. Since that time, Payzant has enjoyed an effective relationship with the mayor, who has oversight responsibility for the public schools. They support each other both publicly and privately, and their positive relationship has done a great deal to tone down the political rhetoric that can often bog down big-city education reform efforts.

After less than a year as superintendent, Payzant released a forty-four-page document, *Focus on Children*, which laid out a five-year reform plan for the city's schools.[4] Since the plan's release, BPS has been active in its campaign to implement the *Focus on Children* directives. Principally, the central office has developed a series of standards for all major subjects, including English and language arts, mathematics, social studies, science, and even guidelines for school-to-career and the arts.[5] BPS has also instituted benchmark exams, a system of accountability pegged to these standards.

In addition, BPS, in collaboration with the independent group Boston Plan for Excellence, has installed literacy and math coaches in many of the city's schools.[6] These individuals are responsible for coordinating the professional development, assessments, and other practices deemed necessary to improve teaching and learning. BPS has also adopted a policy of requiring all principals to form an instructional leadership team in their school. In short, BPS, at the central office level, has been aggressive in developing policies and practices that will work to bring the *Focus on Children* goals to life.[7]

In addition to BPS's commitment to promoting educational achievement, part of what has driven the Boston school reform effort in the past three years is the mandate from the state to meet state-defined standards (around which the BPS standards now revolve). As of 2003, the state will require all students to have passed the tenth-grade state standards-based examination, the Massachusetts Comprehensive Assessment System (MCAS), to earn a high school diploma. (The first class of tenth graders required to pass the MCAS exam in order to graduate took the test in spring 2001.) Given that such a high percentage of BPS tenth graders have not passed this test (40 percent failed the English/ language arts portion and 47 percent failed the math portion in 2001), the city is under enormous pressure to bring its students up to the levels of achievement demanded by the state.[8]

The mayor takes the lead

In order to broaden community commitment, enhance student achievement, and move the reform agenda forward, Mayor Menino launched at the beginning of his second term (1998) a series of non-BPS-based initiatives that would support the schools and children's learning.[9] Perhaps the most significant venture, and the one most germane here, began with a declaration made in 1998 in his second inaugural address. In the speech, Menino announced the opening of a new office in City Hall: the Boston 2:00-to-6:00 After-School Initiative.

In many ways, the creation of this office was the culmination of years of work by grassroots organizations involved in the after-school field. One such group, Parents United for Child Care (PUCC), had been working as an advocate for the children of Boston since the 1980s by leveraging a continuum of capacity-building resources for hundreds of youth-serving programs. PUCC took the lead on a number of initiatives during the 1990s that began the complex process of both raising the profile of after-school programs and, more important, building more comprehensive support for them. For example, Boston was one of three cities chosen in 1995 by the Wallace–Reader's Digest Funds and the National Institute on Out-of-School Time (NIOST, located at Wellesley College) for a project to improve after-school programs. Employing a community-based collaborative approach to improving the quality and quantity of out-of-school services, the project (Making the Most of Out-of-School Time, or MOST) sought to develop systematic means of coordinating the after-school activities in the city and furnishing training for after-school providers. In addition to providing technical assistance to particular programs, the project funded slots for programs through affordability grants. Mayor Menino served on the MOST advisory board, and it was this project that first garnered his serious attention to after-school programs.

Having an office in City Hall to highlight and drive an agenda to expand after-school opportunities for children was, for the whole after-school field, a significant step toward increasing the visibility of this effort and resources for it. The pressure to expand and improve the field was now elevated, in part because such change was tied to the fortunes of the mayor. More important, the office was a welcome addition because it brought with it the capacity to help leverage new funds to support programs, coordinate the opening of school facilities in which programs could operate, and work to develop citywide infrastructure to support programs over the long term.

Menino hired Jennifer Davis, a former deputy assistant secretary for the Office of Intergovernmental and Interagency Affairs under U.S. Secretary of Education Richard Riley (and the first author of this chapter), to head the Boston 2:00-to-6:00 After-School Initiative (also known as the 2:00-to-6:00 Office). With a small staff and limited budget, the 2:00-to-6:00 Office began its work and soon learned the difficult challenges associated with the mayor's stated goal "to offer a quality, affordable after-school activity in every neighborhood to every child who wants it."[10]

Early work of the 2:00-to-6:00 Office

Early progress involved overcoming some of the chief obstacles standing in the way of developing a citywide system of delivering quality after-school programs. The first and most basic hurdle was obtaining more complete information than existed at the time about how many programs there were, where they were operating, and how many children they served. PUCC had begun the very complicated process of gathering this information from licensed after-school programs through its annual *Guide to Boston's Before and After School Programs*. In Boston, as in most other cities, after-school programs seemed to have sprung from highly localized needs rather than from one coherent strategy, so mapping them would be a challenge. Because there was no centralized waiting list for programs, parents would need to be surveyed directly to gauge the demand in the city for after-school programs.

To assist in this project, the 2:00-to-6:00 Office secured the pro bono services of a private consulting firm and a private survey research firm. These firms brought powerful tools and talents to the task and, because of the data they produced, imparted a new legitimacy to the field of after-school programming. They completed work in March 1999, reporting that approximately sixteen thousand elementary and middle school children in Boston were enrolled in after-school programs. At least an equal number desired to be in a program, but programs were not available.

Mapping the field was an important first step toward finding ways to make programs affordable and available in every neighborhood and promote more efficient use of resources. Another significant step toward increasing the number and size of after-school programs was the mayor's commitment to pay for additional costs to keep school buildings open until 6:00 P.M. This policy had the immediate effect of multiplying the number of programs that operated in the schools. Indeed, in his State of the City Address in January 1999, the mayor announced proudly, "In less than a year, we've increased the number of school-based programs by nearly 50 percent," and the number has increased since then. As of fall 2001, sixty-nine schools (of a possible one hundred elementary and middle schools) had full-time after-school programs, most of them operated by community-based organizations such as the YMCA, the Boys and Girls Clubs, Citizen Schools, the B.E.L.L. Foundation, and New England Scores.

As impressive as this expanding connection between schools and after-school programs was (at least in terms of physical space), the mayor insisted that the 2:00-to-6:00 Office held a broader mission than just promoting the sharing of facilities. In the same State of the City Address, Menino declared, "This year after-school programs that we fund must begin to *reinforce the school curriculum*. And we will insist on quality control."[11] In addition to demonstrating the mayor's commitment to education, this mandate also reflected parental concerns, as the survey of parents conducted on behalf of the 2:00-to-6:00 Office had revealed that parents believed that academically focused activities in after-school programs were among the most important. Given the disparate missions and activities of the over 240 programs in Boston, however, forging ahead with a centralized initiative to strengthen program quality would prove to be a complex endeavor.

Focus on learning outcomes

While the 2:00-to-6:00 Office brought a fresh face (and considerable leverage) to this challenge, many after-school providers, the higher education community, ReadBoston and various cultural institutions (including the Children's Museum, the New England Aquarium, and the Boston Museum of Science) had for years been working with children during nonschool hours to provide tutoring and experiential learning. In the years immediately preceding the formation of the 2:00-to-6:00 Office, several new after-school entrepreneurs had created programs that placed the objective of improving student learning as one of their central goals. Furthermore, there were several BPS schools that had begun to connect more closely to the after-school programs operating in their buildings.

Some model programs and schools

Three of the newer after-school programs are particularly worth mentioning. The first program to come into existence was the Steppingstone Foundation. Founded in 1990, the Steppingstone Scholars Program is a fourteen-month-long tutoring and support program for students from disadvantaged neighborhoods in Boston. The goal of the program is to help the students gain admission to premier public high schools like Boston Latin and Latin Academy or an independent school by teaching them the skills that they need to succeed.[12] The tutoring takes place during two intensive summers and two afternoons per week and Saturdays throughout the year. While public school students spend 1,080 hours per year in class, Scholars have an additional 540 hours of class time.[13]

The second program, the B.E.L.L. Foundation, was founded by a group of Harvard Law School students in 1992. The current mission is "to increase the academic achievements, self-esteem and life opportunities of elementary school children living in historically underserved communities." Its participants spend many hours in extra tutoring in math and reading in order to supplement the learning in the BPS.[14]

Finally, Citizen Schools began in 1995 as an after-school program model that links experiential education with academic outcomes for participants, with a specific focus on developing students' math, writing, and oral presentation skills. It operates on an apprenticeship model, bringing in community volunteers who contribute their professional and life experience to the teaching that takes place.[15]

Yet even programs that attempted to align their activities with BPS's learning goals often found it difficult to get clear feedback from teachers and school staff around how to structure this alignment. This reaction from BPS was not universal, however; a number of BPS schools were pioneers in connecting their work more closely to after-school programs. One of the most advanced is the Gardner Elementary School, located in the Allston section of Boston. Headed by an activist principal with a clear vision of how her school could become a full-service institution for the neighborhood, Gardner worked in partnership with Boston College and the YMCA to bring this vision to life. The school offers children after-school opportunities in many areas, from painting to homework assistance to karate. Although only a third of students now participate in these programs (due mostly to funding and transportation limitations), the principal's goal remains that of having every child enrolled in these programs, for she recognizes that the more time children spend in productive activities, the more likely they are to succeed academically. Not coincidentally, the Gardner's MCAS scores have seen one of the highest improvement rates in the state.

But a model like the Gardner was not the norm. Traditionally, most out-of-school programs incorporated homework help and literacy support into the programs, but reinforcing specific curricular features of school, like mathematics, or connecting closely to the activities of the school day seemed beyond the scope of what after-school programs could do. Also, schools usually perceived the after-school field as a wonderful support system that was distinct from schools in its relaxed settings and its deliberate lack of formal methods (such as tests and grades) to measure achievement. Most educators believed that without the more prescribed elements of learning that characterized school, after-school programs could not help promote the kinds of academic success that formal schooling was being held accountable for.

Expanding Youth Horizons Initiative

To support the efforts of after-school programs to strengthen learning, the 2:00-to-6:00 Office launched the Expanding Youth Horizons Initiative in 1999. Its first undertaking was a conference co-organized with the Boston Children's Museum and supported by a wide range of partners, including individuals from a number of after-school providers (like the Boys and Girls Clubs and the YMCA), researchers, and representatives from BPS. Over three hundred after-school providers attended. The mayor and Superintendent Payzant each delivered keynote addresses making the case for the importance of after-school programs in reaching their overarching goal of advancing the learning and development of children in the city. The event's workshops were designed to equip providers with information, skills, and materials needed to help them support children's learning in fun and creative ways, focusing on literacy, math, and science.

The central document distributed at the conference detailed materials summarizing the key concepts of the BPS and state standards in literacy, mathematics, and science according to grade level. Written with the help of a BPS teacher and the curriculum directors for literacy, math, and science, the document juxtaposed those standards with activities characteristic of after-school programs that would act to reinforce and deepen these concepts. As the book explained in the introduction, "While school teachers have the primary responsibility for helping children succeed academically, after-school time offers a unique opportunity to focus on creative learning activities that can help children build skills in an environment that supports overall healthy social development."[16]

Other learning-focused initiatives

Other initiatives taking place in Boston helped to reinforce and build on the 2:00-to-6:00 project. The 4 Quality Initiative—a collaboration of the Boys and Girls Clubs of Boston, NIOST, PUCC, and the YMCA of Greater Boston—is one such program that brings training, technical assistance, and system building to the field, so that it will be better equipped to serve as a partner with schools in promoting learning. The 4 Quality Initiative is grounded in research that establishes the valuable contribution of after-school programs to the healthy development of children and youth and identifies the link between staff training and program quality. For example, the initiative furnished staff and administrators at the YMCA and Boys and Girls Clubs with four-day training session workshops on balanced programming, standards for learning, developmental needs of children and youth, and thematic curriculum development. Participants develop their knowledge in these areas in training focused thus far on homework assistance, science, literacy development, the arts, and numeracy and math. The project intends to transfer its practices and lessons learned to the larger field to assist a much wider range of programs.

Another initiative is a model of providing after-school education from a youth development perspective. Responsive Advocacy for Life and Learning in Youth (RALLY) is an in-school and after-school program that operates as a partnership between the host schools (two are in Boston, a third is in the planning stage in Boston, and the program is replicated in other cities as well), the Harvard Graduate School of Education, McLean Hospital/Massachusetts General Hospital/Harvard Medical School, and a network of community organizations, such as the YMCA and Boys and Girls Clubs.[17] Essential to this model is that after-school staff serve additional functions: several times a week, they work in children's classrooms for part of the regular school day, and they are trained and supervised by clinicians to develop supportive relationships to enhance the resilience of at-risk youth. Out of this work, a mental health training and learning initiative has emerged, supported by the Harvard After-School Initiative and the Harvard Program in Afterschool Education and Research. Thus, some after-school staff serve as "prevention practitioners," pulling supports into the school and after-school classroom rather than pulling children out for specialized services. Practitioners work with teachers and administrators in middle schools to become integrated into the school environment and coordinate their students' school experience with their after-school experience. They help students build strong relationships with adults and peers and get the academic support they need, targeting the most intensive services for those most in need. They also provide after-school programming and facilitate collaboration among schools, families, after-school and community programs, and social service agencies to help ensure that children are ready to learn. This program has shown strong outcomes for participating children.

Boston Community Learning Centers

The federal 21st Century Community Learning Centers program (known in Boston as the Boston Community Learning Centers, BCLCs) also played a significant role in the expansion of educationally oriented after-school programs in Boston. Since the original grant in 1998 and a state grant to support the BCLC model, two more rounds of CLC grants have brought the total number of sites operating in the city to thirty, serving an estimated twenty-five hundred children. The BCLCs are managed through the city's Office of Community Partnerships, which has been thoroughly committed to the goal of connecting after-school to the school day.

One way the BCLCs have focused their work on promoting academic achievement was to participate in a state-designed pilot project with the specific purpose of inducing or improving communication and collaboration between the school-day teacher and after-school staff. Known as the cross-fertilization project, this initiative paid teachers a stipend to spend time in after-school programs and after-school staff to spend time in school classrooms. Over the spring, the teams of teachers and teams of after-school staff met to develop a summer curriculum for the after-school program that integrated the BPS learning standards into the activities of the after-school program.[18]

The BCLCs have also helped to strengthen the commitment of BPS to building its infrastructure to support after-school programs. An important practical and symbolic step forward is paying for two staff people to work directly in the BPS central office (in the office of the assistant director of curriculum and instruction) on BCLC projects. One of these projects is a series of free citywide trainings for after-school staff (of any programs, not just those operating in BCLC sites) that explain how after-school programs specifically might structure their activities to support the BPS learning goals.

These trainings, called "Bridging the Gap," are in strong demand; several sessions have been conducted multiple times in order to accommodate program provider interest.

These various initiatives indicate the creativity of Boston programming but also the complex challenge of creating an integrated structure.

Two civic initiatives

On the macro level, two significant advances that helped to shift perceptions about the role of after-school programs came through some unique partnerships and commitments on the part of Boston's civic leaders. Although challenges were associated with both initiatives, they ultimately played a substantial role in moving Boston toward its goals.

Mayor's Task Force on After-School Time

After the consulting firm completed its report on the status of the after-school field in Boston, Mayor Menino sought to bring together civic leaders from various constituencies to design a vision for the future of after-school programming in Boston. He and the 2:00-to-6:00 Office also believed that they would not be able to advance the goals of the field without first forming a consensus around a ten-year vision for building an after-school system in Boston, designing a specific set of recommendations on how to get there, and bringing a broader group of stakeholders to the table.

The mayor appointed Chris Gabrieli to head the Mayor's Task Force on After-School Time. Gabrieli, a Boston businessman, had strong roots in the philanthropic community and a keen interest in education. The mayor knew that his commitment to civic life and his leadership skills could help create a new civic commitment to the mission of the 2:00-to-6:00 After-School Initiative. Mayor Menino convened the task force made up of leaders from business, K–12 education, higher education, after-school providers, child care, criminal justice, human services, and the philanthropic sector. It began its work in June 1999.

The task force deliberations were at times acrimonious as members came to the table with divergent perspectives on the purpose of after-school programming. Debates on the issue resulted in two very important agreements. First, the members developed a shared ten-year vision for after-school programming in Boston. This vision was approved very early in the life of the task force and provided the foundation for all its future work. The second agreement was the adoption of an outcomes model based on the framework developed by the Carnegie Council on Adolescent Development in 1989. This framework, which classified the five developmental needs of children (cognitive, social, physical, spiritual and moral, and emotional), demonstrated how after-school programs can and do help address these needs.[19] With all members embracing this framework, the task force ensured that it would deliver its report to the mayor as a unified group.

In May 2000, the task force released its report, entitled *Schools Alone Are Not Enough: Why Out-of-School Time Is Crucial to the Success of Our Children*, which argued forcefully that "academic support during out-of-school time will be a critical factor determining whether Boston rises to this challenge [of meeting the state standards]. . . . *Out-of-school time must be elevated to true peer status with school hours.*"[20] Its list of over twenty recommendations integrated a wide variety of ideas and called on a number of key municipal and community-based institutions to lend their expertise and resources to the effort. The recommendations included appealing to the city, state, and federal government to increase funding directed to after-school programs; asking civic leaders to launch a statewide publicity campaign to promote the need for high-quality after-school programming; and developing a pilot project to implement an outcomes-based system of program implementation in order to measure more directly the impacts of after-school programs on children and their families.[21]

This report instantly became a blueprint for how the after-school community in Boston would move forward in the effort to coordinate its diverse activities. In addition to energizing the field, its most immediate contribution was to prompt the second major civic action to cast the learning aspect of after-school programs in the spotlight. This initiative took the learning goals agenda to the next level by institutionalizing it within the funding community.

After-School for All Partnership

After his work on the task force, Gabrieli devoted nearly all of his time to the after-school issue. Together with the original director of the 2:00-to-6:00 Office, he founded a nonprofit organization, Massachusetts 2020, in October 2000. The former director of the 2:00-to-6:00 Office became the organization's president; Gabrieli served as chairman. This group's mission was to serve as a catalyst organization for increasing after-school programming in Boston and around the state and raising the profile of the issue of using nonschool hours as a prime learning opportunity. Following up on one of the major recommendations of the task force report, Gabrieli secured the formation of a partnership of Boston-based funders "to develop and implement a coordinated strategy to support after-school programming."[22]

In March 2001, ten months after the release of *Schools Alone Are Not Enough*, Mayor Menino and Gabrieli announced the formation of the Boston After-School for All Partnership (ASAP), the largest public-private partnership devoted to children in Boston's history. The partnership took shape around three goals: expanding the number of children served by five thousand slots in five years, raising the learning outcomes of Boston's students and developing more sustainable sources of funding. Included in the fourteen-member partnership are such major organizations as the Nellie Mae Education Foundation, Harvard University, FleetBoston Financial Foundation, and the United Way. With the weight of over $24 million over five years (including $5 million in City of Boston funds) committed to the three specific goals, the partnership helped to crystallize the vision of a strong collaboration between after-school programs and schools.

Even with the significant funding and influential players now involved in the effort to develop a systemic approach to after-school programming, however, the partnership still faces monumental challenges. How will the field become coordinated to meet the demand better? How will the partnership bring its collective resources to leverage a much larger financial commitment from public sources? Some basic organizational questions that underlie these grand questions also linger. How will program providers be encouraged to focus on explicit learning goals? How will the partnership work with after-school providers, city staff, and the BPS to encourage policies and practices to connect the aims of after-school programs more closely with those of the public schools? Still in its infancy, the partnership has begun the hard work of addressing these and other matters.

Transition to Success pilot project

By looking closely at one learning-oriented program, the challenges and successes of connecting after-school programs more closely to the schools becomes evident. In spring 2000, using city funds, monies from the Massachusetts Department of Education specifically targeted to after-school programs, and funding from Massachusetts 2020, the Boston 2:00-to-6:00 After-School Initiative launched the Transition to Success (TTS) pilot project.[23]

Pilot project beginnings

The primary purpose of the TTS pilot is to connect a particular group of BPS students to high-quality after-school programs and also provide them with outreach and support geared to increase family and parent involvement and the students' overall academic and social success. Three essential project elements are worth noting. First, its target population is the most academically at-risk students (as identified by BPS).[24] This focus has strong implications for its potential success as a model: that the central goal of the participating after-school programs is wholly aligned with that of BPS, that is, raising the benchmark scores of the most academically at-risk children. Even more important, almost universally, these children had not participated in any after-school programming at all prior to their involvement in the pilot. Now these children would have a quality place to go after school.

Second, the TTS pilot pays for a coordinator at each of the participating sites. This coordinator is responsible for monitoring the services received by the students and serves as the main line of communication between the program, the school, and parents regarding students' learning and overall development. Ultimately, then, the coordinator must address students' nonacademic barriers to success in order to help students achieve academically. Finally, in the true spirit of public-private partnerships, the 2:00-to-6:00 Office has partnered with Massachusetts 2020 to operate the pilot.[25]

After identifying six participating sites through a competitive request for proposals process, the project began in January 2001 with 105 students and ran through the end of the school year.[26] One notable success of this half-year speaks to the effort of the pilot to put mechanisms and a strategy in place that would guide the participating programs toward practices that would enhance children's learning outcomes. For three months, under the guidance of an evaluation and consulting team, the sites worked together to develop a logic model (see Figure 4.1). The model captured the coherent flow of particular program activities into inducing certain specified outcomes identified by program staff as key to program success. The intent of the model was to enable program staff to focus on how their daily activities produce particular outcomes and converge to lead to improved student achievement. With this logic model in place, the six programs could, as the year progressed, design activities that would deliberately produce particular outcomes and more effectively integrate the goal of improved student learning into the daily operations of the program.

Figure 4.1. Transition to Success logic model

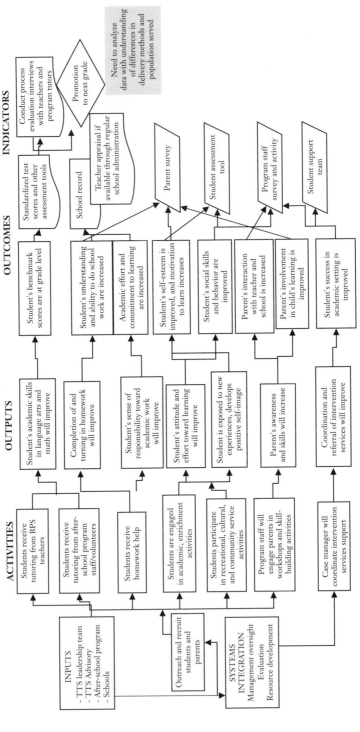

The pilot project: The first full year

The first full year of the TTS pilot project has revealed both the great promise of this outcome-focused program improvement plan but also the substantial obstacles to success. On the positive side, the most significant contribution has been to involve those academically at-risk children in quality after-school programs at all.

In addition, the focus on increasing parental involvement has had largely positive outcomes. Preliminary surveys show that 98 percent of parents are satisfied with their child's after-school program. Perhaps even more important, 88 percent of parents agree that the after-school program helps them to connect with their child's teachers. Programs have found that for a variety of reasons, parents of BPS Transition students seem to be more detached than other parents from their children's schools, so such a strong indication of involvement with children's formal education is a considerable victory.

A second achievement is illustrated by the meaningful steps that programs have taken to help programs address more fully the academic needs of participants. One program instituted a homework journal, for example, where students, tutors, and staff could chart progress and setbacks on various subjects. This practice has had two important effects. First, the time dedicated to homework completion was enhanced as a learning opportunity rather than just an activity that took place before the "real program" began. Second, these journals have become a vehicle through which to communicate with the students' teachers directly. In turn, through the homework journal, teachers identify key areas where students need extra attention; thus, students' particular learning needs are addressed, and school professionals are included in the after-school program. In fact, the program that initiated the homework journal reported such strong outcomes that other TTS pilot sites will begin to institute this practice as well.

The TTS pilot has also had its share of obstacles. The most frustrating has been the fact that communication between teachers and after-school staff, the linchpin in connecting the work of each, has been erratic. Deeper communication between teachers and after-school staff around teaching strategies and curriculum coordination has yet to take place across all sites. Teachers must sacrifice their few moments of free time during the day in order to make coordination happen, and only a few teachers have been persuaded that this sacrifice will pay off. Most do not yet believe that time spent communicating with after-school personnel will necessarily facilitate progress toward their own student learning objectives.[27] What may be needed is a kind of cultural shift within the educational establishment that incorporates the idea that time spent in after-school programs is not superfluous, but rather can have a direct impact on academic achievement. If teachers were provided financial incentives to engage in this kind of collaboration, they would also be more inclined to value it.

Whether programs meet the expectations of the logic model, whether the programs improve qualitatively as a result of the pilot, and whether the model of having a staff person devoted to the needs of particular students can be deemed successful is still largely undetermined midway through the pilot. The hope is that the evaluation of the pilot (slated to be complete by midsummer 2002) will demonstrate the broader impacts that these after-school programs can have.[28]

Conclusion

For a number of reasons, the future prospects for systemically joining after-school programs into a true partnership with BPS schools to enhance children's learning and overall development are bright. The mayor and philanthropic and other civic leaders are firmly committed to this goal and are investing new financial and leadership resources to attain it. Those working directly with children must surely be boosted by the fact that their work is encouraged by many of the city's most powerful people. Second, many programs and schools have taken great strides toward working together. The time seems not far off when these models become the norm, and the message that after-school programs are integral to education reform will at last penetrate completely. The fundamental challenge ahead is for the BPS, civic and private sector leaders, and key stake-holders from the after-school sector to develop and implement a specific and intelligent plan that can realize the vision articulated in the task force report. "In 2010," the members declared, "after-school programming in Boston [will be] recognized as a 'system' in the best sense of the word—one that is flexible and entrepreneurial, responsive to families and communities, and integrated, efficient, and accountable."[29] With all that has happened so far and all that is poised to begin, their vision seems entirely possible.

Notes

1. National Commission on Excellence in Education. (1983). *A nation at risk: The Imperative for Educational Reform report to the nation and the secretary of education, United States Department of Education.* Washington, DC: Author.

2. Massachusetts Commission on Time and Learning. (1995). *Unlocking the power of time: Final report.* Boston: Author. p. 4.

3. See Olatokunbo S. F. (1998). *Review of extended day and after-school programs and their effectiveness.* Baltimore, MD: Center for Research on the Education of Students Placed at Risk. For specific research studies, see, for example: Partners Investing in Our Community of Kids & Ohio Hunger Task Force. (1999). *Urban School Initiative School-Age Care Project: 1998–99 school year evaluation report.* Columbus, OH: Authors. Gregory, P. J. (1996). *Youth Opportunities Unlimited: Improving outcomes for youth through after-school care.* Manchester: University of New Hampshire. See Baker, D., & Witt, P. A. (1996). Evaluation of the impact of two after-school recreation programs. *Journal of Park and Recreation Administration, 14*(3), 23–44.

4. The plan set as its primary goal "to improve teaching and learning in all of our schools" and identified three "ancillary goals" intended to support the realization of the primary goal: changing the structure of the schools to focus on student performance, providing safe and nurturing schools, and engaging parents and the community in school reform. Boston Public Schools. (1996, Aug.). *Focus on children: A comprehensive reform plan for the Boston Public Schools.* Boston: Author. p. 12.

5. These standards have been widely lauded as being both high and attainable. They predate the content standards set forth by the state—the Massachusetts curriculum frameworks—and essentially embody the content covered by the state assessment exams.

6. The Boston Plan for Excellence is an independent nonprofit organization founded in 1984 to support the city's education reform efforts. It is funded by local corporations and foundations. For more information, visit the group's Web site: http://www.bpe.org/.

7. This instructional leadership team is to be composed of all the department heads—or veteran teachers, in the case of elementary schools—and is charged

with leading the school's effort to implement the "whole school improvement plan" that each school must adopt. For a full description of the various practices and standards the BPS has adopted, visit the BPS Web site, especially, the "Teaching and Learning" section: http://www.boston.k12.ma.us/teach/.

8. As of this writing, the results from the MCAS retest in fall 2001, given to those who failed the spring test, have not yet been released for Boston.

9. Information is available on the City of Boston Web site: http://www.cityofboston.gov/.

10. Menino, T. M. (1998, Jan. 5). *Inaugural address.*

11. Menino, T. M. (1999, Jan. 11). *State of the city address.* Emphasis added.

12. The Boston Latin School is the oldest public high school in America, founded in 1634. In the most recent MCAS exams, the scores of its tenth graders ranked first among all public high schools in the state. The Latin Academy ranked high also, at nineteenth (out of 320).

13. Steppingstone Foundation: http://www.tsf.org/boston/bos-tss.html.

14. B.E.L.L. Foundation. (2000, Sept.). *BASICs 1999–2000: Evaluation report.* Boston: Author.

15. Citizen School: http://www.citizenschools.org/.

16. Abdul-Tawwab, N., & Meranus, J. (1999, Sept. 27). *Expanding Youth Horizons Conference notebook.* Boston: 2:00 to 6:00 After-School Initiative. p. 3.

17. Noam, G. G., Warner, L. A., & Van Dyken, L. (2001). Beyond the rhetoric of zero-tolerance: Long-term solutions for at-risk youth. In Russell J. Skiba & Gil G. Noam (Eds.), *Zero tolerance: Can suspension and expulsion really keep schools safe?* New Directions for Youth Development, no. 92, Winter 2001, pp. 155–182. San Francisco: Jossey-Bass.

18. Interview with Juanita Wade, director, Office of Community Partnerships, Nov. 19, 2001, Boston.

19. These five developmental areas were derived from: Carnegie Council on Adolescent Development & Report of the Task Force on Education of Young Adolescents. (1989). *Turning points: Preparing American youth for the 21st century.* Washington, DC: Author.

20. Mayor's Task Force on After-School Time. (2000, May). *Schools alone are not enough: Why out-of-school time is crucial to the success of our children.* Boston: Author. pp. 2–3. Emphasis in original.

21. Mayor's Task Force on After-School Time. (2000). pp. 6–7.

22. Mayor's Task Force on After-School Time. (2000). p. 13.

23. The state monies were part of the After-School/Out-of-School Time program run out of the Massachusetts Department of Education. The grants were disbursed on a competitive basis and funded programs in over eighty communities across the state. The legislation providing for this program (and earmarking approximately $5 million) included the following language: "Said grants shall fund a variety of activities, including but not limited to, academic tutoring and homework centers, athletic programs, health services, arts programs and community service programs." Massachusetts FY 2001 Budget, line item 7061–9611.

24. The students in the pilot are those identified by BPS as at risk: those who failed at least one of the city's benchmark exams in grades 2, 3, 5, 6, 7, or 8. The so-called transition program (from which the pilot gets its name) deliv-

ers after-school tutoring and in-school assistance to these students with the primary aim of helping them to pass the next round of benchmark exams.

25. Massachusetts 2020 is paying for the evaluation of the students participating in order to track the program impact. In addition, Massachusetts 2020, with a seat on the project's leadership team, shares a role in setting policy for the pilot project and overseeing its implementation.

26. Each after-school program is run by a community-based organization that partnered with its host school to apply for inclusion in the transition pilot. The sites are Hamilton Elementary School–Jackson Mann Community Center (Brighton); Hurley Elementary School–Boston Excels/Home for Little Wanderers and YMCA of Greater Boston (South End); Mattahunt Elementary School–B.E.L.L. Foundation (Mattapan); Josiah Quincy Elementary School–Boston Chinatown Neighborhood Service Center (Chinatown); and Quincy Upper School–Boston Chinatown Neighborhood Service Center (Chinatown).

27. The site using the written reports, for example, admits that the system, which began before the start of the pilot project, was in place nearly two years before most teachers would fill out the form regularly. By all accounts, these teachers have seen this impact through increased homework completion, better class participation, and better attitudes toward learning.

28. The evaluation will look at both quantitative BPS data (test scores and grades) and more qualitative, personality-based issues like self-esteem, leadership skills, general behavior, and motivation for learning. When combining the student's self-evaluation with the evaluation of both parents and that of the after-school staff, evaluators expect to be able to produce a fairly detailed portrait of each student's psychological and learning profile. Furthermore, evaluators will have access to two comparison groups through which to analyze the impact of the after-school program. The first group is the participants themselves, as students, parents, and staff will complete two sets of surveys: one near the outset of the program and one at the conclusion. By comparing the profiles rendered at the beginning of participation to those rendered at the conclusion, evaluators will have a direct line to judge how involvement in the program affected change in individual students. Second, evaluators will have access to quantitative data for all transition students throughout BPS, and so will be able to hold the larger sample, without guaranteed participation in after-school programs, up against the TTS pilot group, which was able to participate in these high-quality programs.

29. Mayor's Task Force on After-School Time. (2000). p. 39.

JENNIFER DAVIS, *president of Massachusetts 2020, served as executive director of the Boston 2:00-to-6:00 After-School Initiative from 1998 to 2000.*

DAVID A. FARBMAN *is the research director at Massachusetts 2020.*

San Francisco's Beacon Initiative is designed to foster youth development on a large scale. Its intermediary, Community Network for Youth Development, used a theory of change process to forge consensus and create a road map to guide this large collaborative toward its long-term goals.

5

Building the San Francisco Beacons

Sue Eldredge, Sam Piha, Jodi Levin

THE BELL RINGS; class lets out. Students mill about the hallways, some heading outside, others moving toward a different part of the school. These students filter again into classrooms, perhaps passing their parents as they leave an English as a Second Language or computer training class. The students' options for after-school learning are plentiful: some pick up instruments and costumes for an arts program, others choose to design Web sites in the center's tech labs, while others elect to attend leadership groups or academic tutoring classes. The space feels youthful yet respectful, and definitely comfortable. In this, and at seven other schools in target neighborhoods across San Francisco, Beacon Centers are open, offering youth and their families the opportunity to learn, create, and grow in a safe atmosphere.

For information about Beacon's beginnings, we are grateful for the work of K. E. Walker and A.J.A. Arbreton. Walker, K. E., & Arbreton, A.J.A. (2001). *Working together to build Beacon Centers in San Francisco: Evaluation findings from 1998–2000.* San Francisco: Public/Private Ventures, 2001.

NEW DIRECTIONS FOR YOUTH DEVELOPMENT, NO. 94, SUMMER 2002 © WILEY PERIODICALS, INC.

The impact of Beacon Centers

Each Beacon Center is managed by a lead agency with deep roots in the surrounding community, and dedicated youth workers from local organizations lead all programs and services. To create these learning-rich environments, over one hundred community-based organizations, ten city agencies, and sixteen private foundations collaborate in a complex and challenging initiative guided by an innovative tool, the theory of change. Moreover, the Beacons enjoy strong support from the center's neighbors, political leaders on a local and state level, and influential policymakers. The technical assistance intermediary to the initiative, Community Network for Youth Development (CNYD), forges the strong partnership that governs the Beacons' success and promotes youth development strategies and practices in the hope of producing exemplar sites in the long run.

Eight school-based neighborhood centers operate at sustainable capacity year-round; they are open both before and after school. In 2001, nearly five thousand youth and two thousand adult family members participated in the centers' programs, which consist of an eclectic mix of classes in five programming categories: education, leadership, career development, health, and arts and recreation. The initiative as a whole represents a strong public-private partnership of the San Francisco Unified School District (SFUSD), the San Francisco Department of Children, Youth, and Their Families, the Juvenile Probation Department, and private foundations, which contribute $2.8 million annually to the centers as long as they meet performance standards. From this partnership, $350,000 per site is allotted annually for core funding, creating a robust community platform from which to expand services. This high level of support for the initiative continues despite key personnel changes at the initiative level: three school district superintendents, three leaders of the Department of Children, Youth, and Their Families, two mayors, and private foundation leadership have come and gone during the lifetime of the initiative. Yet evaluators undertaking a multiyear evaluation report that all of the initiative's early goals have been successfully met, with strong inroads being made toward the initiative's intermediate goals.

Setting the stage for success

In San Francisco in the early 1990s, youth in poor neighborhoods had limited access to enriching opportunities and lacked safe places to gather. Meanwhile, across the country in New York City, people who were working to improve the lives of poor urban youth had shared their concerns with those interested in getting adolescents into safe havens after school and found that their solution lay in providing neighborhoods with greater access to school facilities. The City of New York decided to provide grants to create school-based youth development centers—Beacon Centers— that would focus on providing resources to youth in the nonschool hours. In 1994, program officers from three private foundations in San Francisco traveled to New York to learn more about the New York City Beacon Centers. They spoke with staff from the Youth Development Institute at the Fund for the City of New York, the technical-assistance intermediary for the New York initiative. They also toured the centers.

Growth of public commitment

At the same time, conditions were conducive for launching a city-wide initiative to open school-based youth development centers in San Francisco schools as well. The superintendent and staff from the SFUSD were interested in working in greater partnership with the community and using schools in broader capacities. In 1991, San Francisco voters passed a proposition to set aside 2.5 cents per $100 of assessed real property value to support programs for San Francisco's youth. The Office of Children, Youth, and Their Families (now the Department of Children, Youth, and Their Families) was designated to administer the funds. Coleman Advocates for Children and Youth, which spearheaded the creation of the Children's Fund, encouraged the city of San Francisco to fund and support the Beacon Centers.

In fall 1994, full of enthusiasm for the possibilities, staff from the SFUSD, the Department of Children, Youth, and Their Families, and the Evelyn and Walter Haas, Jr. Fund formed the Beacon

Steering Committee (BSC) to create the San Francisco Beacon Initiative. (The BSC continues to serve to this day, providing overarching policy and funding leadership.) The steering committee brought together a broad-based planning group of about thirty people who met consistently over the course of a year to plan the initiative. The group was made up of city officials, representatives from the school district, service providers, representatives from Coleman Advocates, parents, and technical assistance agencies, including CNYD, at that time a small agency providing youth development training and support to youth-serving agencies in the San Francisco Bay Area.

Shaping the approach

The planning group shaped the San Francisco adaptation of the New York Beacon model. As in New York, San Francisco's Beacon Centers would be neighborhood youth centers designed from a youth development approach. They would seek to engage the strengths of the surrounding neighborhood in the support of young people; they would be available to youth of all ages in their neighborhoods, not just youth at risk; and they would provide a broad range of activities that emphasized supports and opportunities key to promoting healthy youth development:

- A sense of emotional and physical safety
- Supportive relationships with adults and peers
- Opportunities for meaningful participation and sense of belonging
- Community involvement
- Skill building through interesting and challenging learning experiences

Recognizing that youth need continuity of supports and opportunities throughout their development, Beacon Centers would become permanent community resources, with secure annual core funding. In the San Francisco model, the centers would be developed in full partnership with a local public school, which would provide space, utilities, and janitorial support. Each center's lead agency would be community based and provide fiscal and administrative management, as well as convene other youth-serving agencies to bring their talents and knowledge to the centers. Finally, to attract the commitment of public dollars, private foundations would bring flexible money to the initiative for start-up costs, technical assistance, and evaluation. Federal and local public agencies would then provide long-term funding for service delivery to the neighborhoods.

The intermediary

As the steering committee began to unfold the initiative, members realized the need for a strong technical assistance team—an intermediary—that would bring leadership in concert with the initiative's youth development mission and provide staff support and management expertise as it began to implement the initiative. It was decided that CNYD, already a respected resource for youth development capacity building, would serve in this critical role.

"We wanted some kind of neutral body," said Sylvia Yee, vice president of the Evelyn and Walter Haas, Jr. Foundation and founding member of the BSC. "We needed an entity that wasn't going to be of the public sector, or the private sector, because we wanted to set this up as something that was owned by the community. We didn't just want to offer more resources to kids after school; we wanted to benefit from the best thinking about youth development programming. And CNYD had already done a lot of work in this area."

CNYD's first task as intermediary was to assess the challenges. The BSC was charged with funding and policymaking for the overall initiative. Community sites were made up of community and school staff, and each had their own needs and demands. As intermediary, CNYD was nebulously charged with a guiding leadership role but without decision-making authority. Each stakeholder had its own priority outcomes and often had unrealistic expectations for impact. How would CNYD forge agreement about initiative goals? How would it set appropriate developmental expectations for growth and progress?

CNYD staff also knew they would need a great deal of public commitment for the centers to succeed. What resources did they have available, and what might they have in the future? How could they ensure sustainability, and how many sites could they mount and sustain over what time period? What level of public commitment, and from whom, would be needed? And how could they mount the necessary evidence to show that investments were having their intended impact?

Beyond these crucial management and planning issues, the immediate concrete task was to provide the needed support for the start-up of the first two Beacon Centers. The planning group had developed the general parameters that Beacon Centers would conform to, and the BSC launched the implementation phase by selecting sites and lead agencies for the Beacon Centers. Communities with the greatest need were identified based on the challenges faced by their young people and their families and the level of local resources available to provide ongoing support to the centers. School sites and agencies in those neighborhoods were considered on the basis of their history in the community, the strength of their leadership, and their readiness to implement the Beacon model. Two agencies met all criteria and were selected to develop the first two Beacon Centers by spring 1996. Two more centers would follow soon after, and another four centers would be added by 2000 in distinct neighborhoods of need.

Launching phase: Laying track while the train is moving

Because both planned Beacon Centers were in Empowerment Zones (areas that receive federal support to attract new business and housing), CNYD had expected that federal funds would constitute the bulk of the start-up funding. But in 1995, the U.S. Congress, at that time led by Congressman Newt Gingrich, announced large reductions in social spending. The opening of one of the centers was delayed, and initiative leaders hoped to raise the dollars for annual core operating expenses from local funds administrated by the San Francisco Department of Children, Youth, and Their Families. Leaders also decided to phase in sites more slowly and to ensure that sustainable local funding for existing sites was secure before approving any expansion.

Using the theory of change process

Program staff from private foundations began to press for the initiation of an evaluation that, once implemented, would provide the needed evidence for local funding. As staff searched for evaluation resources, they came across the work of the Aspen Institute Roundtable on Comprehensive Community Initiative. In 1995, the Aspen Institute published *New Approaches to Evaluating Community Initiatives*, a report that furthered the concept of using a theory of change—or, "a theory of how and why an initiative works"—as a standard against which to measure the success of comprehensive community initiatives.[1] Carol H. Weiss, a professor of education at Harvard University, introduced the theory of change in 1972:

The concept of grounding evaluation in theories of change takes for granted that social programs are based on explicit or implicit theories about how and why the program will work. The evaluation should surface those theories and lay them out in as fine detail as possible, identifying all the assumptions and sub-assumptions built into the program. The evaluators then construct methods for data collection and analysis to track the unfolding of the assumptions. The aim is to examine the extent to which program theories hold. The evaluation should show which of the assumptions underlying the program break down, where they break down, and which of the several theories underlying the program are best supported by the evidence.[2]

In her preliminary work with the theory of change, Weiss evaluated programs in retrospect, after they had been planned and implemented. In *New Approaches*, the authors proposed that there were good reasons to begin the design and evaluation of an initiative with a theory of change. They argued that it could sharpen the planning and implementation of an initiative, facilitate the measurement and data collection elements of an evaluation, and reduce problems associated with causal attribution impact by articulating a theory of change at the outset of the initiative and gaining agreement on it by all stakeholders.[3]

As a planning tool, the theory of change allows users to define the necessary phases of development from early, to intermediate, to long-term outcomes. Participants begin with their long-term objectives and then map backward, outlining each action necessary to bring them to their goal. Each action is then submitted to three crucial tests:

- Is it plausible? (Will the initiative's activities lead to desired outcomes?)
- Is it doable? (Will the resources be available to carry out the initiative?)
- Is it measurable? (Can an evaluator track the initiative's process using its theory of change?)[4]

CNYD staff immediately grasped that the theory of change process could provide answers to the initiative's challenges by providing a tool to engage the diverse stakeholders, as well as to design the complex organizational structure by which it could be managed. CNYD contracted with James P. Connell, coeditor of *New Approaches* and director of the Institute for Research and Reform in Education (IRRE), to create the San Francisco Beacon Initiative theory of change. The process was conducted in two phases: an early phase in which outcomes were defined and the resources required to obtain them, and a later phase in which the indicators for measuring success were determined. In all, this process took over a year to complete.

Setting outcome goals, identifying priorities

To begin, CNYD staff conducted one-on-one interviews with steering committee members, executive directors from the two lead agencies, and school principals, youth, and family members from the two sites. They asked about their interviewees' vision of what a successful Beacon Center would look like five years into the future and what kind of place would attract neighborhood youth and have impact on their lives. From these interviews, a researcher from IRRE developed the Beacon story, a narrative of what initiative stakeholders hoped to achieve and how they expected to arrive at their goals.

CNYD staff then gathered the BSC and site leaders together to review the Beacon story. It was clear that a multitude of interests and perspectives had been captured. The story also showed that stakeholders expected that the Beacons would promote significant change in four separate yet interconnected domains (youth development, family support, school reform, and community development). It was evident to everyone that achieving equal impact in each domain was neither plausible nor possible given the level of available resources.

CNYD staff then worked with stakeholders to prioritize their outcomes. Stakeholders decided that creating a place where young people would flourish was the most important outcome of the initiative. Thus, youth development was affirmed as the core of the Beacons work and given the greatest weight when allocating resources. Staff incorporated family support, school reform, and community development—and their own belief that each must be supported to provide a healthy arena for youth—into the outcomes as well and drew an image to exemplify their interdependency. A concentric circle surrounding the target—youth development—represented each priority (see Figure 5.1).

Figure 5.1. Targeting resources

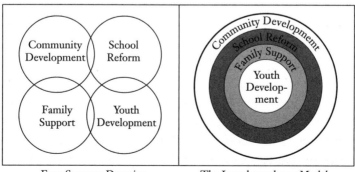

Four Separate Domains   The Interdependency Model

Once the hopes and aspirations of community members and funders were captured, CNYD staff began to flesh out the theory of change. Over many meetings, CNYD asked stakeholders to address the question, "What must we do in order to achieve our long-term goals?" and translated their answers into achievable early, intermediate, and long-term outcomes. They also defined what the indicators of success would be and how each stakeholder would know when they had accomplished these incremental outcomes.

New stakeholder roles

CNYD staff next identified the human, financial, material, and political resources necessary to ensure that the outcomes were plausible, possible, and measurable and who would provide these resources: the Beacon sites themselves, the intermediary, or the members of the BSC.

If the Beacon Centers were to achieve full scale, representing a significant and permanent community resource, all partners would need to do business differently (see Table 5.1). The BSC would be asked not only to fund the initiative but also to guide and support the Beacon Initiative by setting policy, sustaining yearly core funding, promoting public support of the initiative, using their influence to negotiate systems-level accommodations and agreements, and assisting in leveraging funding from diverse sources. Community stakeholders would be asked to work for the larger good of the entire initiative in addition to addressing the needs of their own Beacon Centers. The public school system needed to broaden its academic focus and support the partnership by drawing on a larger vision of youth development and community participation.

The final product from the theory-of-change process was a map of the responsibilities of the three stakeholder groups (now formally known as site level, initiative level, and intermediary) as they progressed through three distinct phases to the initiative's long-term goals. Each stakeholder level was responsible for ensuring that certain designated outcomes were achieved during each phase (see Figure 5.2).

Table 5.1. Community stakeholders' roles

Partner	Traditional Role	New Role
Public-private funders	Award funds	Pool resources for coordinated distribution
	Use own grant-making processes and monitor those grants as a single entity	Develop and use a shared grant-making process and accept common biannual reports
	Provide short-term funding (one to three years)	Commit to long-term funding
	Allow funded agencies to operate according to their own guidelines	Establish policies and guidelines for the initiative
	Resist using their influence on behalf of an organization	Negotiate needed operational accommodations from institutional partners
Service providers	Compete with other local CBOs to serve as primary service provider	Work with other local CBOs and community agencies to provide services using shared resources and drawing on a shared youth development vision
Schools	Self-manage after-school programs or allow space use by others	Partner with community agencies to develop a Beacon Center; provide leadership and support; work to leverage additional state and federal funds to expand and sustain Beacon programming
	Serve only students who attend the school	Serve children, adolescents, and their adult family members from the surrounding neighborhood

The Beacon theory of change

According to the Beacon theory of change, Beacon Centers would reach their long-term outcomes only if their early and intermediate outcomes had been met. Specifically, site-level staff would first need to encourage community engagement and leadership; create centers that were visible, safe, accessible, and welcoming; hire staff who were well trained, diverse, and responsive; and provide programs that supported their long-term outcomes. (Table 5.2 provides examples of strategies that sites took to meet early outcomes.) At the initiative level, the BSC focused first on raising the required

Figure 5.2. San Francisco Beacon Initiative: Theory of change

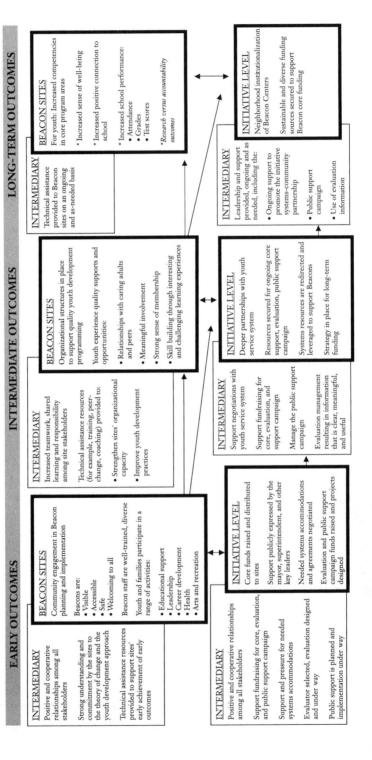

EARLY OUTCOMES

INTERMEDIARY

Positive and cooperative relationships among all stakeholders

Strong understanding and commitment by the sites to the theory of change and the youth development approach

Technical assistance resources provided to support sites' early achievement of early outcomes

BEACON SITES

Community engagement in Beacon planning and implementation

Beacons are:
• Visible
• Accessible
• Safe
• Welcoming to all

Beacon staff are well-trained, diverse

Youth and families participate in a range of activities:
• Educational support
• Leadership
• Career development
• Health
• Arts and recreation

INTERMEDIARY

Positive and cooperative relationships among all stakeholders

Support fundraising for core, evaluation, and public support campaign

Support and pressure for needed systems accommodations

Evaluator selected, evaluation designed and under way

Public support is planned and implementation under way

INITIATIVE LEVEL

Core funds raised and distributed to sites

Support publicly expressed by the mayor, superintendent, and other key leaders

Needed systems accommodations and agreements negotiated

Evaluation and public support campaign funds raised and projects designed

INTERMEDIATE OUTCOMES

INTERMEDIARY

Increased teamwork, shared learning and responsibility among site stakeholders

Technical assistance resources (for example, training, peer-change, coaching) provided to:
• Strengthen sites' organizational capacity
• Improve youth development practices

BEACON SITES

Organizational structures in place to support quality youth development programming

Youth experience quality supports and opportunities:
• Relationships with caring adults and peers
• Meaningful involvement
• Strong sense of membership
• Skill building through interesting and challenging learning experiences

INTERMEDIARY

Support negotiations with youth service system

Support fundraising for core, evaluation, and support campaign

Manage the public support campaign

Evaluation management resulting in information that is clear, meaningful, and useful

INITIATIVE LEVEL

Deeper partnerships with youth service system

Resources secured for ongoing core support, evaluation, public support campaign

Systems resources are redirected and leveraged to support Beacons

Strategy in place for long-term funding

LONG-TERM OUTCOMES

INTERMEDIARY

Technical assistance provided to Beacon sites on an ongoing and as-needed basis

BEACON SITES

For youth: Increased competencies in core program areas

• Increased sense of well-being
• Increased positive connection to school

• Increased school performance:
  • Attendance
  • Grades
  • Test scores

Research versus accountability outcomes

INTERMEDIARY

Leadership and support provided, ongoing and as needed, including the:
• Ongoing support to promote the initiative systems–community partnership
• Public support campaign
• Use of evaluation information

INITIATIVE LEVEL

Neighborhood institutionalization of Beacon Centers

Sustainable and diverse funding sources secured to support Beacon core funding

Table 5.2. Beacon Center strategies

Early Outcomes:

Beacon Center Characteristics	Examples of Strategies Employed
Engage community	Use multiple strategies (advisory councils, surveys, focus groups, family dinners, town hall meetings) to gather ongoing community and participant input and engage community residents through employment and volunteer activities.
Safety	Employ and train community workers as safety and support staff to monitor entrances and hallways, interact with participants, and respond to threatening situations.
Visibility	Conduct ongoing outreach to neighborhood residents and ensure good signage outside and on the school facility.
Accessibility	Offer programming at times that are most useful for participants (for example, for adult family members who requested access to programs during the day when their children are in school).
Welcoming	Engage youth in the creation of a youth-friendly space, and employ staff and volunteers who speak the native language of the participants and live in the neighborhood.
Diverse and well-trained staff	Employ a diverse staff and provide baseline training and supervision to all staff and volunteers to ensure consistency in promoting safety and positive developmental experiences.

core funding, using their institutional influence to broker the needed agreements and accommodations among systems-level players, and seeking funding for a public support campaign and evaluation to promote long-term public commitments to the initiative.

High-quality experiences for youth

The theory of change postulated that in order to achieve long-term outcomes, site leaders must, in the intermediary phase, shift their focus to strengthening their organizational capacity and program practices to ensure consistent and high quality in all their programs.

(Quality is defined by those features that research states are crucial to positive youth development.) CNYD believed that practice that promoted quality developmental experiences for young people would be the critical bridging outcome that would allow young people to succeed in many realms, including school achievement. The theory furthermore predicted that quality programming would also serve to attract and sustain the participation of young people and their families over time. Ensuring a deeper level of participation would also result in young people at the Beacons using more of their discretionary time in safe and productive ways.

At the initiative level, the BSC was charged with deepening relationships with the greater youth service system, continuing to forge necessary system accommodations that would allow the Beacon sites to function at high levels, and developing long-term strategies for stable core funding.

The Beacon theory of change ultimately predicted that if the intermediate outcomes were achieved, young people would demonstrate increased competencies in the core program areas and would experience an increased sense of well-being, positive attachment to school, and better school performance. If the initiative-level stakeholders were successful at securing sustainable core funding for the Beacon Centers, the theory of change predicted that the centers would become permanent resources within their neighborhoods.

The need for community collaboration

The Beacon Initiative theory of change further postulates that the leaders at the community and systems levels cannot create the change necessary to achieve their goals for young people without acting together. In fact, accountability for successfully achieving the outcomes at one level was conditional on the success of the other level in meeting its outcomes.

For example, in the early phases of the initiative, initiative-level stakeholders were accountable to garner the support of the mayor, school superintendent, and private foundations; successfully negotiate the needed space and custodial agreements with the schools;

and pass these resources on to the site-level stakeholders. The site-level stakeholders were then responsible to create the needed partnerships with their school and neighborhood and build centers that would attract large numbers of neighborhood youth and their families. Only then could the initiative-level stakeholders move to the next task: securing the commitment of city decision makers for stable core funding and negotiating the redirection of other existing resources for the expansion of Beacon Centers.

This interdependency between system and community stakeholders continues into the intermediate phase. For example, often when there are staffing and personnel changes at the site level, earlier agreements between the Beacon Center and the school have to be renegotiated. When this does not happen smoothly, there can be tension between the staff of the school sites and the Beacon Center that disrupts the functioning and operation of the center and impedes progress toward outcomes. These transitions are left to the sites to navigate first, but when accommodations cannot be reached, school site and Beacon Center staff alert initiative-level leaders, and they negotiate accommodations to ensure progress toward the outcomes.

The intermediary's tool

The theory of change required that the intermediary provide leadership and management for the initiative as a whole and technical assistance to each of the centers to meet their program and operational goals, and then assist the BSC by managing many of its projects, such as the evaluation, the public support campaign, and the solicitation of private funds. What CNYD found was that the theory of change, in addition to outlining responsibilities, became the most important tool for management, planning, and implementation.

During the early planning and start-up phase, the theory of change enabled CNYD to create a compact between stakeholders to proceed on a mutually agreed-on path. This compact afforded CNYD the unspoken authority to direct the initiative's resources in the service of moving down that path. CNYD's continuing ability to lead was the result of its success in forging sound agreements, collective commitment, and a strong sense of mutual accountability among the large number of diverse stakeholders, all guided by the theory of change.

As the initiative began to develop the next six sites, the theory of change served as a critical tool to manage their unfolding implementation. In yearly initiative-wide planning retreats, CNYD used the theory of change to reflect on the progress made in the past year. Staff compared the theory of change guidelines with their actual progress, and if they were not where they expected to be, they recalibrated plans and, as needed, resources, for charting future progress. Because of the developmental structure embedded in the theory of change approach, CNYD has been able to encourage leaders to approach what they do as a work-in-progress and to attend to the incremental accomplishments that serve as the stepping-stones to long-term outcomes. The theory of change also allowed CNYD to keep funders' expectations real, as it mapped exactly what they could expect and when they could expect it. This was critical to hold their attention, interest, and patience, as many were accustomed to having less involvement with their grantees and providing them with shorter-term funding commitments.

Evaluation

Early in the initiative's life, large sums of money were being committed to the centers, and investors wanted to know that their funds were making a difference in communities. CNYD also needed to show its public supporters that the initiative was having impact. Both were imperative reasons to begin an evaluation, and CNYD had to raise a substantial amount of money to evaluate an initiative of the Beacon's scale and complexity. The theory of change allowed CNYD staff to lay out what they wanted evaluated and to interest funders in investing in an outcomes-based evaluation. It also served to put stakeholders, rather than the evaluators, in command of what was being evaluated.

CNYD ultimately employed two teams to evaluate the initiative. Public/Private Ventures is midway through a four-year evaluation that assesses how successful the initiative has been at reaching the early and intermediate outcomes. In its interim evaluation report, which focuses on years two and three of Beacon implementation, Public/Private Ventures found that CNYD successfully achieved its early outcomes (building and establishing five Beacon Centers, engaging a diverse and representative number of young people, and providing comprehensive programming). Milbrey McLaughlin and a team of Stanford University graduate students are conducting a smaller evaluation that focuses on understanding the impact of the Beacon experience on a representative group of Beacon students.

Lessons learned

There are three important insights to share on some of the most valuable learning over these first five years:

• *Build on the knowledge and resources of others.* CNYD owes a great debt to the New York Beacons and the wisdom and knowledge that so many people shared in shaping the San Francisco Beacon Initiative. The initiative moved more quickly by adapting New York's approach to meet San Francisco's needs and resources than if something entirely new had been created. When CNYD was looking for ways to approach the evaluation, staff looked at what research and practice had to say about what was working for other comprehensive initiatives, and this brought them to the Aspen Institute's work and the theory of change. They then brought in an expert, James Connell, who supported CNYD staff as they underwent this process.

CNYD chose to create its own theory of change because at the time, the youth development field was not as developed as it is now and an external theory of change was not available. However, the process of creating the Beacon Initiative theory of change was long and arduous, and although it did create for the stakeholders a sense of ownership, we believe that it is not necessary to create a theory of change anew to get this degree of buy-in so long as stakeholders know they can have a significant effect on a theory's design and change it when necessary.

• *A strong theory of change binds stakeholders to outcomes over time.* When an initiative aims at creating permanent resources, long-term core funding is required. Early on, CNYD decided not to make the mistake of assuming a "pilot" mentality: that is, if there is ample funding for the first three years of work, the sites will prove their worth and attract ongoing sustainable funding while still maintaining integrity to their outcomes. CNYD asked that funders commit for the long term, and the theory of change proved that their dollars would provide an incredible, and long-lasting, array of opportunities for San Francisco's young people to learn and grow.

• *A theory of change is a tool that evolves and deepens over time.* Perhaps because the process goes by the name of "theory," CNYD staff expected that they would create their theory of change in its totality at the outset and that it would remain static, just as a scientific theory would. In fact, it became clear that a theory of change should be a malleable and changing document because learning occurs as the initiative is created, and this must be reflected in any theory of change. For example, discussion of early outcomes, strategies, and resources were real to stakeholders when they were in the midst of establishing new Beacon Centers, but it was difficult for them to engage in discussions of intermediate and long-term outcomes. Now, as the early outcomes are complete and the concentration moves to meeting intermediate outcomes, CNYD will engage stakeholders in a reassessment of the intermediate outcomes and take a deeper look at the strategies and resources needed to achieve them.

And, as always, external conditions affect what can be delivered. For example, federal and state after-school dollars are flowing into the Beacon Centers, but there is a great deal of pressure for the Beacons to concentrate on educational enrichment activities to help boost school performance. All of the sites are adjusting to this pressure by ramping up their focus on educational programming while, with the support of local dollars, maintaining programming in the areas of leadership, career development, health, and arts and recreation.

Most of the local private funders have generously supported the initiative and the sites over the past five years, but will they continue to fund? And if private or public funding declines, are there other funding sources that can be garnered, especially in a time of economic downturn? How must the theory of change adjust to prepare for this possibility? In two years, San Francisco will have a new mayor, who will appoint the head of the Department of Children, Youth, and Their Families. How will CNYD build the community support that will enable continued funding for the Beacons through this transition? CNYD is in the midst of finding answers to these questions; it is and will be an ongoing process. To the degree the theory of change can be used as a tool for stakeholders to examine their process, change course as needed, and recommit to providing San Francisco's youth with positive resources for learning and growth, the Beacon Centers have the greatest possibility of moving forward with success.

Notes

1. Weiss, C. H. (1995). Nothing as practical as good theory: Exploring theory-based evaluation for comprehensive community initiatives for children and families. In J. Connell, A. Kubisch, L. Schorr, & C. H. Weiss (Eds.), *New approaches to evaluating community initiatives: Concepts, methods, and contexts.* Washington, DC: Aspen Institute.
2. Weiss. (1995).
3. Connell, J. P., & Kubisch, A. C. (1998). Applying a theory of change approach to the evaluation of comprehensive community initiatives: Progress, prospects, and problems. In K. Fulbright-Anderson, A. C. Kubisch, & J. P. Connell (Eds.), *New approaches to evaluating community initiatives: Theory, measurement, and analysis.* Washington, DC: Aspen Institute.
4. Connell & Kubisch. (1998).

SUE ELDREDGE *is the executive director of Community Network for Youth Development, San Francisco.*

SAM PIHA *was the managing director of the San Francisco Beacon Initiative for the first five years of the initiative's development. He is the current director for Community School Partnerships at Community Network for Youth Development, San Francisco.*

JODI LEVIN *is a freelance writer and editor.*

San Diego is the first major city in the nation to provide free before- and after-school services to every public elementary and middle school within its borders.

6

San Diego's 6 to 6: A community's commitment to out-of-school time

Deborah Ferrin, Steven Amick

SAN DIEGO's 6 to 6 Extended School Day Program is the legacy of former mayor Susan Golding, who envisioned opening every one of San Diego's 202 elementary and middle schools from 6:00 A.M. to 6:00 P.M., to make them available to students during the hours that most parents work. A single parent, Mayor Golding was passionate about providing safe extended-school-day supervision to all children and youth in the community. As a policymaker, she focused her efforts on public schools, located in every neighborhood and supported by taxpayers, which were being used only from 8:00 A.M. to 3:00 P.M. As national movements to reform welfare, education, and juvenile justice systems converged to make after-school funding a priority, Mayor Golding in 1995 convened the Safe Schools Task Force, a collaboration of local policymakers, to develop a plan that would ensure that San Diego was poised to take a leadership role in the after-school arena.

NEW DIRECTIONS FOR YOUTH DEVELOPMENT, NO. 94, SUMMER 2002 © WILEY PERIODICALS, INC.

Implementing a citywide plan

This intergovernmental Safe Schools Task Force, consisting of the superintendent of schools, school principals, a county juvenile court judge, juvenile probation officers, the city manager, the city attorney, and chief of police, developed three goals for the safety of students in San Diego: closing high school campuses during lunchtime, strictly enforcing curfew and truancy laws, and creating the 6 to 6 Extended School Day Program. Entering the 1998–1999 fiscal year, as the city was struggling to balance a $47 million deficit, Mayor Golding fought to include $1.75 million in the budget, which financed the first thirty-one elementary schools to receive the program. The budget was passed on June 28, 1998, and the new school year was scheduled to begin just two months later, on August 28, 1998. That is when I (Deborah Ferrin), as the city's child care coordinator, was assigned the task of making the program operational. I asked how many schools the mayor would like to see operational in the first phase of implementation. Her response was that she wanted them all open on the first day of school and for all staff to be prepared to respond to the media. I obtained a list of principals' home phone numbers and kept calling until thirty-one agreed to participate.

Public-private partnerships and unprecedented collaboration

There was general agreement between the city and the school district that neither entity could implement the program as expediently or cost-efficiently as community-based organizations (CBOs). We conducted an extremely fast request for proposals process, allowing respondents a little more than two weeks to prepare their applications. A review panel of school administrators and youth service professionals selected the grantees, and we quickly developed contracts with the agencies selected to provide the services. On

August 28, 1998, the first day of school, all thirty-one sites were operating at full capacity by the end of the day.

This success was the direct result of the history of collaboration that had existed in the San Diego community for years prior to the implementation of San Diego's 6 to 6. CBOs such as the YMCA of San Diego County, Social Advocates for Youth, and Harmonium all had long histories of developing public-private partnerships to provide quality, licensed school-age care on many of the San Diego City School campuses. These agencies put their full resources behind the program's initial efforts and continue to be the primary provider agencies today, operating 144 of the 202 programs.

The city's initial investment in San Diego's 6 to 6 provided the leverage needed to solicit funds from California's newly developed After School Learning and Safe Neighborhoods Partnerships Program, which was allocated $50 million for the 1999–2000 fiscal year. The process of applying for these funds resulted in an unprecedented level of collaboration in San Diego County. Led by a local advocacy group known as the Children's Initiative, seventeen local school districts, all eager to apply for after-school funds, agreed to collaborate rather than compete and submitted one joint application through the San Diego County Office of Education. The strategy paid off: each of the seventeen school districts received a portion of the funds, with San Diego's 6 to 6 growing from thirty-one sites to sixty-four in its second year.

The city's unique partnership with San Diego City Schools has proven quite successful. San Diego's 6 to 6 was initiated with city funding and administered by city staff. When the district became eligible to apply for state and federal education funds, it became more efficient for the district to pass these funds through to augment the city's existing infrastructure rather than retain the funds and reinvent the wheel. This agreement was documented in the form of a memorandum of understanding in August 1999, designating the city as the fiscal and administrative agent and the school district as the facilities and instructional agent.

We have since replicated this agreement with eight other school districts. Each of these districts already operates fee-based, high-quality before- and after-school programs. Rather than reinvent their wheels, we opted instead to offer each school a $10,000 annual scholarship subsidy in order to include the students for whom the existing programs were cost prohibitive. This model exists in 20 elementary schools, while the remaining 182 sites offer fully subsidized before and after school programs.

Curriculum and delivery

The program curriculum has evolved, building on years of CBO expertise in the delivery of high-quality enrichment activities to elementary students. Credentialed teachers have been incorporated into the after-school programs (two per elementary school, working on the CBO payroll) to ensure that high-quality academic assistance is also provided. The 6 to 6 curriculum seeks to foster a combination of academic skills and developmental assets and includes homework assistance, targeted tutoring, visual and performing arts, science labs, computer training, sports leagues, leadership development, and character education.

The inclusion of middle school students posed a challenge initially, but by adopting a market-driven approach to curriculum development for that age group, middle schoolers were soon attending San Diego's 6 to 6 in high numbers. The successful middle school programs rely more heavily on the faculty, building on relationships that exist between students and the "cool" teachers during the regular school day. Teachers are allowed to teach their passion after school, offering a wide variety of extracurricular activities, augmented by CBO staff. Once these enrichment activities develop a strong following, core curriculum tutoring and homework assistance can be gently integrated into the program and treated as "payment" for the opportunity to participate in the enrichment classes. This might sound like a bait-and-switch scheme, but we promote it as a "special introductory offer" to help our customers, the students, recognize the value of the program. The strategy works.

The program has faced many challenges during its rapid expansion from 31 sites in September 1998 to 196 sites in the fall of 2000. Of these, our efforts to gain access to classroom space have resulted in some of our most creative solutions. During the first year, the programs had access only to auditoriums, cafeterias, and other multipurpose spaces not designated for classroom instruction. In some schools, where auditoriums were divided into classrooms to comply with California's class size reduction policy, programs were held outdoors, in covered lunch arbors. During the second year, districts agreed to provide one classroom for every twenty students enrolled in the program, in addition to indoor multipurpose spaces, libraries, media centers, and computer labs. We thought our problems were solved, but as principals began searching among the faculty for volunteers to share their space, they did not find many who were willing. If we wanted to use classrooms, we had to figure out how to make sharing mutually beneficial.

Two creative solutions have been effective in gaining access to the classrooms of teachers not on our payroll. First, we offer $100 gift certificates to learning supply stores, referred to not as a rental fee but as a "materials replacement stipend." Second, CBO after-school staff arrive on campus one hour before the end of the school day: one hour of their time is traded for an afternoon of classroom usage. This solution has resulted in the development of relationships between teachers and after-school staff that have helped to dissuade fears and foster mutual respect. Ultimately, we believe that most classroom space issues will be alleviated through the natural attrition of teachers over the next ten years. Many of the newly hired teachers come into the job with after-school experience and with an understanding that their classroom will be shared with after-school staff.

We learned quickly that happy principals make for successful programs. Although San Diego's 6 to 6 does not burden principals with the responsibility of administering the program, they have the right to make changes. Also, 10 percent of the program slots are left to the principal's discretion. The program eligibility process focuses on three criteria: full-time employment, eligibility for free or reduced-cost meals, and a commitment to daily participation. Families who meet all three criteria are the highest priority for enrollment. However, principals are often privy to extenuating family circumstances that are not considered in our criteria, and they may override the enrollment system as necessary. At the most successful sites, the 6 to 6 site supervisor is, for all intents and purposes, a member of the faculty; these supervisors may have more day-to-day contact with principals than with their CBO employers. Some principals were initially concerned about having the program on their campus, but most soon found that the program yielded unexpected benefits. One principal noted that "families have returned to their neighborhood school, rather than transfer out, based on the availability of child care."

Standards and evaluation

San Diego's 6 to 6 now serves twenty-five thousand students annually, but the emphasis is not strictly on quantity. All subcontracts with CBO providers require that they adhere to high standards regarding staff qualifications, health and safety training, adult-to-student ratios, incident reporting, and attendance tracking. These standards were designed in consultation with the CBOs themselves, which were insistent that this program adhere to the same levels of quality for which their agencies were known. The city monitors each site a minimum of two times per year for contract compliance, and CBOs conduct internal monitoring visits at least once each month. The city also conducts monthly staff development trainings, offering tracks designed for support staff and supervisors, and using key CBO staff as trainers. Recently, San Diego's 6 to 6 was the subject of an independent evaluation conducted by WestEd (a nonprofit research, development, and service agency), which indicated that its health and safety standards are on par with those of fee-based, licensed school-age programs.

The evidence of this collaboration's outstanding work is in the evaluations conducted over the past two years. A recent study, conducted by Hoffman, Clark & Associates, examined the academic performance of 6 to 6 participants. This research indicated that 57 percent of the students sampled increased their Stanford Achievement Test Series, ninth edition, scores in reading and 44 percent improved their math scores. An annual satisfaction survey of the key stakeholders found that among principals, 91 percent gave the program a favorable rating. In addition, 99 percent of parents, 95 percent of elementary students, and 94 percent of staff rated the program as "good" to "outstanding." Even 88 percent of the program's toughest critics, the middle school students, indicated that they liked coming to the program.

Benefits and challenges

The benefits of San Diego's 6 to 6 are evident on many levels. First is the impact on the students themselves, who are increasing their academic skills and developing positive relationships with caring adults. Second is increased public safety; increased supervision leads to a decreased risk that students will be the victims or perpetrators of crime. The San Diego Police Department's 2001 Crime Index Report indicated that while crime overall was up 8.8 percent compared to 2000, juvenile arrests during the after-school hours were down 13.1 percent. Police chief David Bejarano specifically cited 6 to 6 as one of the primary factors in this decrease. The report also indicated that juvenile victims of violent crime during after-school hours fell 11.7 percent from the previous year. Finally, there is economic benefit to the families both using and employed by the program, removing the need for costly child care on school days and allowing both parents to work full time. One parent wrote to us, "This program has taken a large burden off my shoulders. I now do not have to worry that my son is safe while I am at work. All of my relatives work and there is no one to help me."

One of the challenges is recruiting and retaining quality staff, given the low compensation and lack of benefits for part-time workers. In the spring of 2000, as this program was poised to expand from 64 to 196 sites in the third year, we were grappling with the question of how to increase our staff from 350 to over 1,000 in four months. During the same time period, San Diego City Schools made a decision to reallocate Title I funds by terminating 600 instructional assistants in favor of hiring 200 new teachers. Along with their pink slip, each of these 600 individuals received a tactfully worded invitation to apply for employment with San Diego's 6 to 6.

To maximize retention, we have taken two important steps. First, we mandate that all site supervisors be hired as full-time, benefited employees. This not only adds value to their hourly rate, but allows them time to become part of the regular school day milieu. Second, part-time support staff are given the opportunity to participate in the AmeriCorps Challenge Program, which provides a $2,363 educational trust fund to any after-school worker who completes nine hundred hours of service at the same site during a school year.

Another ongoing challenge is the massive data collection responsibilities. Accurate and thorough attendance tracking is critical to the program, because the provider agencies are paid in accordance with their cumulative program attendance, at a reimbursement rate of five dollars per student per day. In the first two years, we operated a pen-and-paper system that resulted in about seventy-five pounds of entirely accountable but practically useless data. In year three, we purchased computers for all of sites and developed a user-friendly attendance spreadsheet program that collected all the data required. This system, however, had no disaggregation capabilities for detailed evaluation. Entering our fourth year, we now use a comprehensive database software program, and one of the provider agencies has begun experimenting with a Web-based system. We hope to have an entirely paperless system in the future, with parents and staff "signing" students in and out with personal identification codes by electronic time clocks.

We have experienced a tangible paradigm shift in a community that has come to recognize that it does indeed take an entire village to raise its children. Schools cannot meet all students' needs alone and have learned to accommodate and appreciate the assistance of nondistrict staff. CBOs have learned a new way of providing school-age care with less autonomy and a greater emphasis on academic achievement. Cities and counties now subscribe to the notion that after-school is not outside their jurisdiction, but is in fact an integral part of health and human services and public safety. It takes people of vision and commitment to step outside bureaucratic boundaries and embrace change on a broad scale, and we have them in San Diego.

The new challenge lies in truly meeting the goal of after-school for all. San Diego's 6 to 6 provides services to twenty-five thousand children and youth, but another fifty thousand young people wait for the program to grow large enough to serve them. Although 6 to 6 is open 204 days per year, there are another 50 workdays on which it is closed. And although the program has secured $17 million in funding, another $30 million would be required to make latchkey children a thing of the past in San Diego. We have made historical strides, bolstered by strong community support and steadfast political will, and we believe that the full promise of this goal is within reach, through a collaborative investment of public and private resources.

DEBORAH FERRIN *has served as the City of San Diego's child care coordinator since 1990.*

STEVEN AMICK *has administered San Diego's 6 to 6 Program since 1999.*

The long-term success of out-of-school-time pro-
grams may be in jeopardy if they cannot build and
sustain a committed and competent workforce.

7

Out-of-school-time programs:
At a critical juncture

Joyce Shortt

THE UNPRECEDENTED interest in after-school programming in the
past years has spurred an accompanying rise in expectations for
what it might accomplish. Only 20 percent of the waking hours of
children and youth is spent in school, leaving 80 percent of their
time open for extracurricular risk or opportunity. Parents, many
without partners or with limited financial resources, are increasingly challenged with professional and personal demands and dwin-
dling free time, as they try to address the new social realities and
temptations that their children face every day. With the growing
public focus on reducing juvenile crime, keeping young people safe
after school, and boosting academic achievement, out-of-school
time (OST) is being viewed as the new universal remedy.

Positive results, significant challenges
A growing body of research links participation in OST programs
to more positive outcomes for children and youth. Local organizations in areas from the largest cities to the smallest neighborhoods
in the country host OST initiatives because they believe that the

NEW DIRECTIONS FOR YOUTH DEVELOPMENT, NO. 94, SUMMER 2002 © WILEY PERIODICALS, INC.

benefits of such programs reach far beyond the individual to touch the larger community. With a bipartisan national call to community service from politicians as well as religious and community leaders gaining more credence in the post–September 11 era, the field of out-of-school time is poised for success.

Inroads have been made into coordinated, citywide strategies and cross-city communication about OST. For example, the National Institute on Out-of-School Time (NIOST) coordinates the Cross-Cities Network, bringing together leaders from twenty-five city-wide after-school initiatives in major cities across the United States. The three primary goals of this project are to increase the capacity and knowledge of high-level leaders, improve the effectiveness of citywide after-school initiatives, and contribute to the development of a coherent vision for the field at the national level.

Supported by these and other efforts to build and coordinate the field of OST, programs have reached a critical juncture on the path to becoming a nationally recognized foundation of support for young people, along with families, communities, and schools. However, the long-term success of OST programs themselves may be in jeopardy.

OST programs cannot produce positive results without the most critical element in program quality: a committed and competent workforce. Experts and advocates alike agree that youth are best served by program staff who are well trained, well compensated, and likely to remain in their jobs. Clearly, the ability of these programs to realize their potential depends crucially on their success in building and sustaining a strong workforce structure. This is one of the most striking lessons from the cities involved in the Making the Most of Out-of-School Time (MOST) Initiative.

The MOST Initiative

The MOST Initiative was a seven-year (from 1994 to 2001), multi-million-dollar project supported by the Wallace–Reader's Digest Funds and designed in partnership with NIOST. MOST's purpose was to improve the quality and availability of programming for children and youth in Boston, Chicago, and Seattle during the hours they are not in school. The keystone of the initiative was its unique system-building approach in which each city's universe of after-school programs, resource and support organizations, schools, cultural and religious institutions, colleges, parents, funders, and regulatory agencies connected and worked together toward the common goal to meet the OST needs of children, youth, and families.

This community-based collaborative strategy strives to develop local capacity for leadership, resources, and commitment and ultimately to build a sustainable infrastructure capable of supporting an after-school system. Early on in the implementation of the initiative, it became apparent that staffing issues, including high turnover and lack of unified training and education, presented major obstacles to achieving the program's goals. To address these challenges, each of the MOST cities offers multiple levels of training and professional development opportunities to its provider communities. However, providing access to training and professional development and working to develop leadership could go only so far in each city, hampered by the difficulty in recruiting and retaining a workforce willing to settle for inadequate compensation and few chances for advancement.

The OST workforce, and not only in Boston, Chicago, and Seattle, is in a state of crisis characterized by chronic staff turnover, which can cripple a program's quality, delivery, and outcomes. In addition, the OST field, which represents a part-time job for most of its staff, offers very low compensation and lacks a professional development system unified by a core body of knowledge, a career matrix, a system of training, or a registry of providers.

The information gap

One obvious immediate need is the gathering of information about the staff, programs, and infrastructure of the after-school field, particularly in the following areas:

Staff at all levels: Who they are in terms of sociocultural background, age, education, and career path; their skills and credentials; how they are compensated for their work; how their day-to-day work is organized; their experiences and perceptions of their work; and the kinds of support they need to develop professionally, stay in the field, and establish a career

Programs: What kinds of programs exist; who or what supports them; what their compensation policies and practices are; how they recruit and retain workers; what they do best; and where they need the most improvement

Infrastructure: What entities exist in communities and at the state and national levels to design, fund, maintain accountability for, and sustain high-quality programs; and what the effects are of staff development and stability on program quality and the outcomes for children and youth

It is essential to piece together an accurate portrait of the field and the workforce in order to form a groundswell of public support for the creation of policies that will help to establish OST work as a profession and ultimately maintain more stable programs for children and families.

To that end, with the Academy for Educational Development Center for Youth Development and Policy Research, the NIOST is currently engaged in a national strategic planning process for workforce development across the after-school field. Among its activities are these:

- Finding available data on the workforce and identifying what data are still needed
- Searching out models and best practices in OST staffing, compensation policies, and financing strategies
- Learning from other fields that have successfully professionalized their workforce and raised program quality

The resulting plan, crafted in collaboration with a diverse group of experts, advocates, and stakeholders from around the country, will identify priorities for research, action, and advocacy on the national, state, and local levels. By autumn 2002, a blueprint for improving the staffing and financing of OST programs will be available to enable the many stakeholders (individuals, groups, organizations, and policymakers) to build a system that will better support program staff in meeting the needs of young people.

Our aim is to ensure the future of high-quality after-school programming by investing in its most critical asset. In offering their dedication to the development of children and youth, OST staff members should have opportunities to build their own skills and knowledge as part of a growing field that offers them respect, support, and adequate compensation.

JOYCE SHORTT *is codirector of the National Institute on Out-of-School Time at the Wellesley Center for Research on Women, Wellesley, Massachusetts.*

Municipal officials can take an important role in developing a community-wide after-school system. This chapter examines how mayors and city council members can serve as catalysts for far-reaching efforts that address key challenges.

8

The various roles of municipal leaders

Mark Ouellette, John E. Kyle

WITH AN ESTIMATED eight million school children between the ages of five and fourteen going home to an empty house on a regular basis,[1] almost every city and town in America offers some activities for children and youth during the nonschool hours. Because most of the funding for after-school initiatives does not flow through the city's budget and most of the programs operating in the community are not run out of municipal agencies, many stakeholders do not consider municipal officials as crucial players in after-school programs. Nevertheless, city officials are uniquely positioned to create the framework for community-wide collaboration on which genuine and lasting progress depends.

Municipal leadership as a catalyst

While municipal governments frequently provide some financial support for after-school programs, municipal financing is only one of the roles city officials can play in establishing a citywide youth development system. Mayors and city council members have served

NEW DIRECTIONS FOR YOUTH DEVELOPMENT, NO. 94, SUMMER 2002 © WILEY PERIODICALS, INC.

as a catalyst for far-reaching efforts that address a number of other key challenges:

- Broadening access to ensure that all children, including those from low-income families and neighborhoods, have opportunities to participate
- Promoting partnerships that make it possible to forge a shared vision of after-school challenges and opportunities
- Assessing local resources and needs through surveys and data analyses
- Building public will to sustain a strong role in the development of a local after-school system over time
- Improving quality so that programs effectively deliver on the promises of safety, academic achievement, and cultural enrichment
- Financing a citywide system for after-school opportunities that supports stability and long-term growth

Broadening access

A key goal of any citywide after-school system should be to ensure that all children have access to appropriate programs during non-school hours. If parents cannot afford program fees or there are too few opportunities in their neighborhood, large numbers of children may be left out. When that happens, families and cities both lose. Efforts to broaden access to after-school programs do not presume that all children will or should participate. What is important is that all parents have options so that the needs of their children for supervision, recreation, enrichment, and continued learning are met. By seeking to address major issues of affordability, supply, and transportation, municipal leaders have played key roles in broadening access to after-school programs.

The City of Fort Myers, Florida, is using its Success Through Academic Recreation Support (STARS) program to offer after-school learning and cultural enrichment opportunities in neighborhoods where children have the greatest needs. STARS operates out of a recreation complex located in the heart of the city's minority community, and it supports academic tutoring as well as classes ranging from modern and African folk dance to vocal arts, creative writing, and cultural and heritage arts. With a strong parent involvement component and links to local schools, STARS is cited by the city's police department as a major factor behind a 28 percent drop in juvenile arrests citywide.

Promoting partnerships

An effective after-school system depends on a strong set of community partnerships. They encourage and enable schools and youth-serving agencies to work together in meeting the needs of children and families. These partnerships also provide a framework for engaging other key stakeholders—including police chiefs, business and religious leaders, park and recreation officials, and representatives of major cultural institutions—in collaborative efforts.

In most cities and towns, municipal leaders are the only individuals who can convene these diverse segments of the community and promote a lasting focus on expanded after-school opportunities for all children. Although there will always be differences of opinion and conflicting interests among community partners, mayors in particular can create a climate for progress by clearly articulating their hopes and expectations for cooperation among key agencies and organizations.

Mayor Don Plusquellic of Akron, Ohio, used his 2001 State of the City Address to ask the school district to work with city government in expanding opportunities for community use of public school buildings. The mayor then joined with the school board, teachers, and school administrators to resolve thorny contract issues involving the local custodians' union. As a result of a final contract agreement between the union and the school district, the city is now able to operate after-school recreation and learning programs in a greater number of public school buildings throughout the community.

Assessing local resources

For community stakeholders interested in building a stronger after-school system in their communities, taking stock of opportunities already available to children and youth during nonschool hours is a necessary first step, and municipal officials can be significant partners in carrying out this task. By mapping existing after-school programs, cities can determine what services are in place and where they are likely to be inadequate. By developing partnerships that include municipal officials, stakeholders can expand their access to population and other data, municipal planning and zoning staff, and other resources important to determining what exists and what is needed.

Building public will

Municipal leaders have used their position to educate local citizens and build public will about the importance of after-school programs. Such efforts have publicized the importance of structured activities for children during nonschool hours, increased community and business involvement in after-school programs, promoted partnerships with the public schools, and bolstered public support for new initiatives. As the most prominent individuals in their cities and towns, local elected officials have the unique ability to focus attention on and mobilize support for expanded after-school opportunities for children and their families.

The Salt Lake City Mayor's Office, in partnership with the Salt Lake County Parks and Recreation Department, began offering after-school programs for sixth, seventh, and eighth graders starting in January 2001. YouthCity activities are designed to enrich students through access to artistic, recreational, and technological resources. In addition to workshop space, there is also room for students to study or socialize. Mayor Rocky Anderson has used local and national media events to raise attention to the program. At the 2001 Lights on Afterschool Day, Mayor Anderson outlined a two-year plan for expansion of YouthCity, and he discussed building partnerships with business leaders, nonprofit organizations, and the government to recognize the need to fund programs and provide tax-supported facilities for these programs.[2]

Improving quality

After-school programs throughout a community may be dissimilar (education versus enrichment versus sports focus, for example), but they often face similar challenges. Low salaries and limited hours contribute to staff turnover rates as high as 40 percent and prolonged staffing vacancies.[3] Inadequate training opportunities for providers and lack of clear program standards also pose threats to program quality. The stakeholders and leaders in an effective after-school system recognize that these problems are too large and pervasive for individual programs to solve on their own. Many cities already have a diverse array of after-school offerings in place, including extended-day services at schools and community-based organizations, tutoring and mentoring programs, sports leagues, drop-in programs, cultural and arts activities, and other clubs and instructional activities. What cities frequently need is a support structure for programs that strengthen their capacity to deliver high-quality services to children during nonschool hours. Through leadership and well-focused investments of community resources, municipal officials and community stakeholders can work together to create this infrastructure and steadily improve program quality over time.

In Columbus, Ohio, the Cap City Kids program launched by Mayor Michael Coleman places great emphasis on the quality of the after-school opportunities it provides. Using program standards developed by the Mayor's Office of Education in collaboration with education and community leaders, the city initially supported five pilot sites and examined whether its standards yielded the intended outcomes. After parent and student report cards demonstrated improvement in homework completion, social skills, and stronger connections with adults and caregivers, the city subsequently expanded the program to operate at twenty sites. The Mayor's Office of Education is also working with youth-serving agencies such as the YMCA to encourage the broader use of these standards throughout the community.

Financing a citywide system

A long-term financing plan is essential to the success and sustainability of a citywide after-school system. Cities and their partners within county governments, school districts, community foundations, and local businesses can and should work together to ensure that after-school programs are adequately funded over time.

While most after-school programs rely heavily on some combination of parental fees and state or federal funding, cities that have made the most progress toward sustainability understand that developing mechanisms to finance a citywide system is primarily a local responsibility. Municipal leaders do not have to pay all the bills, but they are able to look ahead and put all the funding pieces together in a way that works for their communities.

First, they can assemble a clear picture of long-term costs. Understanding the costs of a citywide after-school effort at both the program and system levels is a key step in the development of a long-term financing plan. Costs can vary greatly and must reflect both direct service expenses and the necessary ongoing investments in human resources and physical infrastructure.

In addition, they can create a framework for shared responsibility. Recognizing that municipal government cannot do the job alone, cities that secure state or federal funds (or both) and build a solid local funding base for after-school programs are well positioned for long-term success.

Municipal leaders are strong advocates for increased after-school funding at both state and federal levels. They work to ensure that their communities get a fair share of state and federal dollars and push for the opportunity to administer these funds locally.

Furthermore, they use local data to guide future investments. A number of cities, large and small, have developed a "children's budget" to trace the path of every dollar invested by municipal agencies in after-school programs and a wide range of other services for children and youth.

Conclusion

In each of these areas, municipal leaders can play key roles by focusing public attention on key issues, convening major stakeholders, and setting an agenda for citywide progress. The stature and influence of mayors and other city leaders are often essential in order to bring community partners to the table and develop local action plans. When strategizing on designing a youth development system, it is crucial to involve the local elected officials early in the process. Programs that have had sustained success (L.A.'s BEST, Sacramento's Students Today Achieving Results for Tomorrow, and Boston's 2:00-to-6:00 After-School Initiative) included a local elected official early in their design phase.

The National League of Cities' Institute for Youth, Education, and Families has undertaken a three-year project to broaden awareness among municipal officials of the diverse roles they can play to stimulate and support after-school programs, deepen and enhance the involvement of municipal officials around expanded learning opportunities during the nonschool hours, and develop a variety of resources to assist municipal leaders as they seek to improve the quality and numbers of after-school programs in their community.

There are multiple resources available through this National League of Cities project. They include an action kit distributed to municipal officials across the United States, audioconferences open to varied community stakeholders, and technical assistance focused on eight cities designed to help these locations and extract lessons applicable to the broad universe of cities and towns. Although the bulk of the project resources are aimed directly at local elected officials, the project goal also is to conduct outreach to nongovernment leaders at the local level so that they have more information about relevant municipal responsibilities and actions and to signal to those community leaders that local elected officials may be receptive to playing key roles in a citywide after-school system.

Notes

1. National Institute on Out-of-School Time, Center for Research on Women, Wellesley College. (2001). *Fact sheet on school-age children's out-of-school time.*

2. The Afterschool Alliance initiated Lights on Afterschool! in 2000 to call attention to the importance of quality after-school programs in the lives of children, families, and communities. The event is held each year in thousands of communities across the United States. The National League of Cities Institute for Youth, Education, and Families is a national supporting organization of Lights on Afterschool!

3. Halpern, R., Deich, S., & Cohen C. (2000). *Financing afterschool programs.* Washington, DC: Finance Project.

MARK OUELLETTE *is a senior program associate at the National League of Cities' Institute for Youth, Education, and Families.*

JOHN E. KYLE *is the program director for outreach and strategic planning with the National League of Cities' Institute for Youth, Education, and Families.*

The Charles Stewart Mott Foundation and the U.S. Department of Education are engaged in a unique public-private partnership that strives to integrate the assets and flexibility of philanthropy with the breadth of a major federal program to support meaningful after-school programs and school-community partnerships for children, youth, families, and communities.

9

Ensuring quality and sustainability in after-school programs

An-Me Chung, Adriana A. de Kanter, Robert M. Stonehill

IN 1997, THE MOTT FOUNDATION and the U.S. Department of Education entered a unique public-private partnership in support of the 21st Century Community Learning Centers program, a school reform initiative designed to fund public schools after 3:00 P.M., when as many as fifteen million students are home alone and unsupervised after school each day. The program was designed to capture an underused portion of the day and provide additional academics, learning opportunities that complement the school day, mentoring for young people by caring adults in their communities, lifelong learning opportunities for community members, and a safe place to support these activities during the

NEW DIRECTIONS FOR YOUTH DEVELOPMENT, NO. 94, SUMMER 2002 © WILEY PERIODICALS, INC.

before-school, after-school, evening, weekend, holiday, and vacation hours.

A unique, ambitious partnership

By challenging the paradigm of the traditional school day and emphasizing community involvement and lifelong learning, it is believed that this school-based and school-linked initiative can teach us a great deal about how schools can recast the current time allotted for the school day and school year to serve students and their families better. Academic performance will improve, students will be eager to learn, and public education will be more effective. With learning at their core, these comprehensive centers can help address social development and keep children safe, thus helping working parents during after-school hours.

The 21st Century program was not the Department of Education's first foray into providing after-school programs, but it was quickly to become its most ambitious. Prior to the inception of the partnership, the department had supported after-school programs and related initiatives for many years through such programs as Title I (the federal government's largest elementary and secondary education program targeted at poor children and now funded at over $10 billion) and Safe and Drug-Free Schools (the department's program to prevent violence in and around schools, to prevent the use of alcohol, drugs, and tobacco by young people, and to foster a safe and drug-free learning environment that supports academic achievement), but these programs were limited both in whom they served and what they offered. For example, although the percentage of Title I schools offering before- and after-school programs grew from 9 percent in 1991–1992 to 39 percent in 1997–1998, schools that offered extended-time programs typically served a very small percentage of their students in these programs for an hour a day each week. In addition, unlike the 21st Century program, these programs tended to be solely academic and did not offer a comprehensive range of additional services, such as enrichment activities, recreational opportunities, and health and nutritional services.

For the Mott Foundation, which has over sixty-five years supporting school-community partnerships, this initiative represented a catalytic opportunity for after-school programs to become a gateway to community schools and lifelong learning, and advance some of the foundation's long-held beliefs in community education—the process by which schools and communities mobilize their resources around the educational needs of their children, youth, and families.

Thus, grantmaking at the Mott Foundation enables the 21st Century Community Learning Centers program and other major initiatives to promote sustainable, community-driven expanded learning opportunities that support developmentally appropriate cognitive, social, physical, and emotional outcomes, especially for traditionally underserved children and youth.

This unprecedented partnership between the Department of Education and the Mott Foundation established a long-term commitment that innovatively integrated the assets and flexibility of philanthropy into the design and operation of a federal program. This was the Department of Education's first attempt to embed a public-philanthropic partnership into the design and stewardship of a program formally authorized by Congress in law. The result is that the aggregate resources leverage efficiencies and support the full array of services and activities required to ensure that local programs are of the highest possible quality and have the most likely chance of being sustainable over time.

Funding for the initiative comes from both the Department of Education and the Mott Foundation. Activities funded by each partner are explicitly designed to be separate but complementary, with the federal funds supporting direct services to children and the foundation funds focused on quality issues. In particular, the federal funds, which have grown significantly every year since 1997 and now total $1 billion annually, are used to pay for the direct costs of school-based after-school programs, including personnel, supplies, and equipment. Mott Foundation resources, totaling $100 million over several years, are directed toward training and technical assistance, identifying promising practices, evaluation, access and equity concerns, policy, and public will.

Effectiveness of the partnership

The Department of Education and the Mott Foundation thus far have evaluated the success of the partnership through three primary indicators: the quantity of funds available, applications received, and children served; the quality of 21st Century programs funded and applications submitted; and the efficiency of administering services greatly needed by children and their parents.

• *Quantity.* Because the demand for after-school programs far exceeds the supply, growth of the 21st Century Community Learning Centers program is an important indicator of partnership success. The dramatic increase in funding for the program by Congress over the past four years, from $1 million to $1 billion, was stimulated by evidence accumulated and disseminated by the partnership that documented public demand for after-school programs, as well as program effectiveness. The investment in public outreach and planning assistance has resulted in annual increases in the number of grant applications received, from 1,950 in 1998 to 2,780 in 2001. And the sharp rise in program funding has resulted, from 1997 to 2001, in an increase in children served (from 1,000 to 1.2 million), the number of communities served (from 6 to 1,600), and the number of schools established as community learning centers (from 20 to 6,800).

• *Quality.* The quality of programs designed by local communities has also dramatically increased. In 2000, 2,252 applications were submitted, requesting a total of over $1.34 billion. About 1,300 of these applications were of high enough quality to be funded, had sufficient funds been available. In 2001, there were 2,700 applications submitted requesting $1.9 billion in funding. The average standardized score of all applications has increased steadily over the program's history from 72 (in 1998) to 75 (in 1999) to almost 80 (in 2000), most probably attributable to the Mott-funded training that potential applicants received in every state.

The ability of the program to provide high-quality services to so many children is due in great part to the pioneering efforts of the partnership between the Department of Education and the Mott Foundation and the long-standing credibility of the foundation as an advocate in the private sector for community schools. As a result, the partnership can leverage additional private resources and gain access to community leaders with expertise in planning and training. The Department of Education's substantial federal resources, meanwhile, bring large numbers of local educators and other public agencies to the table.

• *Efficiency.* Efficiency is key in the partnership, which operates as a flat organization in order to allow a free flow of information between the Department of Education and the Mott Foundation and to capitalize on each other's institutional strengths. Administrative expenditures are less than half allowed by law (0.7 percent versus 1.5 percent). In part because of the Mott Foundation's investments in training and program quality development, as well as the high-quality staff the program can recruit, far fewer federal program officers (thirteen in all) are needed than is typical for a program of comparable size.

Over four years, the program has greatly expanded the quantity and quality of after-school opportunities without any substantial growth in overhead. Other states and localities are recognizing the efficiencies found in such an organizational structure. For example, California has instituted a training and technical assistance intermediary between the Foundations Consortium and the state department of education in the administration of their state after-school program patterned on the Mott Foundation–Department of Education model.

Similar partnerships are also being developed at the city level across the country. Specific to citywide initiatives, the Mott Foundation and the Department of Education believe that the ultimate sustainability of local programs for children and families will depend on the support of local policymakers and practitioners. Thus, the foundation will continue to support the engagement of both the policymakers and the practitioners at the city level to build comprehensive strategies and funding streams.

Replication of the partnership

The most significant opportunity for replication of this partnership is not only for more after-school programs—after-school as a policy initiative is spreading rapidly, spurred on, in part, by the growth of the 21st Century Community Learning Centers—but for the design of similar large-scale, coordinated alliances between government and philanthropy to address other social concerns. National foundations have historically instigated new programmatic ideas addressing a variety of public policy issues. Typically, foundation funding progresses long enough to support studies, demonstration programs, and often implementation at a few multiple sites. At the same time, government initiatives, while often working on a massive scale, are rarely able to capture the flexibility and efficiency of philanthropy to widely develop quality solutions.

The Mott Foundation–Department of Education strategic alliance has successfully wedded the incubation aspect of philanthropy with the large-scale reach of government, instilling the capacities to develop quality and go to scale in the initial design of this alliance. Thus, this alliance has allowed after-school to secure a prominent place on the American school reform agenda, has stimulated similar after-school partnerships around the country, and has been the model for other government-foundation initiatives.

The California Foundations Consortium is working with state-funded after-school programs and 21st Century Community Learning Centers grantees in California to supplement training opportunities. This was a planned and coordinated activity with the state department of education and the consortium. Similar after-school partnership activities are happening in the New York City schools with Open Society Institute funds and in Boston with funds from the mayor's office and the After-School for All Partnership.

Future plans

In December 2001, Congress reauthorized the 21st Century Community Learning Centers law, making broad changes to the program that may affect quality and sustainability. In providing continued national leadership, the U.S. Department of Education and the Mott Foundation will initiate and promote activities specifically directed at program quality and sustainability. The goal will be to encourage expansion of school-based and school-linked after-school programs as a resource for improving student outcomes and lifelong learning opportunities that may lead to reorganizing the school day and school year to serve children and families better. Some examples of future directions for this work are infusing content into after-school programs that complements the regular school day, documenting student impact and effective practices, developing strategies for parent engagement in a changing socio-economic environment, building school-community partnerships, ensuring access and equity, seeding state after-school networks, building city infrastructures bottom up and top down, harnessing public will, and using technology as a strategy for training and dissemination.

AN-ME CHUNG *is a program officer at the Charles Stewart Mott Foundation.*

ADRIANA A. DE KANTER *served as the special adviser on after-school issues in the Office of the Secretary, U.S. Department of Education, during the Clinton administration.*

ROBERT M. STONEHILL *is the acting director for Academic Improvement and Demonstration Programs in the U.S. Department of Education's Office of Elementary and Secondary Education. He has served since 1997 as the director of the 21st Century Community Learning Centers program.*

Index

141

Back Issue/Subscription Order Form

Copy or detach and send to:

Jossey-Bass, 989 Market Street, San Francisco, CA 94103-1741

Call or fax toll-free:

Phone 888-378-2537 6AM-5PM PST; Fax 888-481-2665

Back issues: Please send me the following issues at $28 each
(Important: please include issue's ISBN)

1. YD _____

_____

_____

$ _____ Total for single issues

$ _____ Shipping charges (for single issues *only;* subscriptions are exempt
from shipping charges): First item: $5.00. Each additional item: $3.00.

Subscriptions Please ❑ start ❑ renew my subscription to *New Directions for
Youth Development* at the following rate:

US:	❑ Individual $70	❑ Institutional $135
Canada:	❑ Individual $70	❑ Institutional $175
All others:	❑ Individual $94	❑ Institutional $209

NOTE: Issues are published quarterly. Add appropriate
sales tax for your state for single issue orders. No sales tax for U.S.
subscriptions.

$ _____ Total single issues and subscriptions (Canadian residents, add GST
for subscriptions and single issues)

❑ Payment enclosed (U.S. check or money order only)

❑ VISA, MC, AmEx, Discover Card # _____ Exp. date _____

Signature _____ Day phone _____

❑ Bill me (U.S. institutional orders only. Purchase order required)

Purchase order #_____

Federal Tax ID 135593032   GST 89102-8052

Name _____

Address _____

_____

Phone_____ E-mail _____

For more information about Jossey-Bass, visit our Web site at:
www.josseybass.com   **PRIORITY CODE = ND2**

Other *New Directions* Titles Available from Jossey-Bass

NEW DIRECTIONS FOR YOUTH DEVELOPMENT: THEORY, PRACTICE, AND RESEARCH
(FORMERLY NEW DIRECTIONS FOR MENTAL HEALTH SERVICES)
Gil G. Noam, Editor-in-Chief

NEW DIRECTIONS FOR CHILD AND ADOLESCENT DEVELOPMENT
William Damon, Editor-in-Chief

as a focused area of study. Considers the broader developmental implications of recent findings and addresses what contextual factors produce variations in family assistance and obligation during adolescence as well as implications for other other aspects of development. *ISBN: 0-7879-5778-X*

CD93 **Supportive Frameworks for Youth Engagement**
Mimi Michaelson, Jeanne Nakamura, Editors
Explores the phenomenon of engagement in adolescence and early adulthood. Examines why young people are drawn to certain areas of work and, once there, what sustains them. Explores the central factors of a supportive family background, mentors or role models, involvement in cooperative activities, cultivation of intrinsic interest, awareness of moral and political issues, and traits such as moral sensitivity and optimism.
ISBN: 0-7879-5777-1

CD89 **Rights and Wrongs: How Children and Young Adults Evaluate the World**
Marta Laupa, Editor
Focuses on the way children and young adults understand and form judgments of right and wrong and examines the ways these judgments are independent yet coordinated. Addresses the formation of judgments of right and wrong within and across different domains of knowledge as well as interrelations or coordinations across judgments of different types. Presents research on judgments of truth and how children distinguish domains of truth. Examines how children judge moral and mathematical rights and wrongs and coordinate them with concepts of authority. Also discusses children's distinction between what is held to be factually true and morally right as well as how they make judgments about moral worthiness and moral obligation.
ISBN: 0-7879-1256-5

CD85 **Homeless and Working Youth Around the World: Exploring Developmental Issues**
Marcela Raffaeli, Reed W. Larson, Editors
Provides a step toward integrating knowledge of street youth into the domain of developmental research. Takes a geographical approach, presenting studies from four different regions of the world: India, South America, Africa, and North America. Explores issues of stress and resilience, cognitive development, identity formation, gender differences, and the development of self-efficacy under harsh conditions. Offers practical guidelines for doing research with street youth, addressing the methodological challenges and ethical issues. Provides a model for understanding homeless and working street youth that synthesizes concerns across disciplines, including medicine and public health, and brings a human rights perspective to the study of impoverished youth.
ISBN: 0-7879-1252-2

CD84   The Role of Peer Groups in Adolescent Social Identity:
        Exploring the Importance of Stability and Change
        Jeffrey A. McLellan, Mary Jo Pugh, Editors
        Enhances our knowledge of the adolescent peer world in terms of
        both interpersonal relationships and social categories. Sheds light on
        an array of questions about adolescent social life, including: How
        changeable is peer group influence over time? Do adolescents iden-
        tify with the crowd to which their peers classify them, or do they
        identify more closely with higher status crowds? How do adolescents
        form alternative groups that resist the cultures of the dominant peer
        group? Does having a sibling or dating partner make a difference in
        other relationships? Illustrates the crucial role that peer relationships
        play in identity formation, and demonstrates the importance of view-
        ing the peer world as a dynamic and changeable place.
        ISBN: 0-7879-1251-4

CD78   Romantic Relationships in Adolescence: Developmental
        Perspectives
        Shmuel Shulman, W. Andrew Collins, Editors
        Examines demographic studies of dating patterns and deals little with
        aspects such as the characteristics or development of adolescent
        romantic relationships. Offers both innovative research and com-
        pelling discussions on adolescent romantic relationships.
        ISBN: 0-7879-4124-7

CD72   Creativity from Childhood to Adulthood: The Developmental
        Issues
        Mark A. Runco, Editor
        Offers a comprehensive examination of how creativity develops from
        childhood through adulthood, exploring a full range of issues from
        the biological underpinnings of creativity across the life span to the
        differences between creativity in adults and children. Topics include
        whether creativity in adults is only different in degree, not in kind,
        from creativity in children; the effects of puberty on creativity; mov-
        ing beyond Piaget to accept divergent, chaotic, and creative thought;
        and more.
        ISBN: 0-7879-9871-0

NEW DIRECTIONS FOR MENTAL HEALTH SERVICES
H. Richard Lamb, Editor-in-Chief

MHS54   Neurobiological Disorders in Children and Adolescents
        Enid Peschel, Richard Peschel, Carol W. Howe, James W. Howe, Editors
        Summarizes scientific data about neurobiological disorders in chil-
        dren and adolescents and discusses treatment approaches based on
        these findings—particularly pharmacological treatments. Recom-
        mends fundamental changes in our society's institutions—including
        the medical profession, the insurance industry, the educational sys-
        tem, and the legal system—necessitated by these findings.
        ISBN: 1-55542-758-8